The French in Our Lives

The French in Our Lives examines the profound influence of French language, culture, and thought in the world and, specifically, on the US and Americans throughout history.

While many books discuss the similarities and differences between the two cultures, this book focuses on the influences – frequently overlooked – of French culture on the US. The insights provided through this examination promote a better appreciation and understanding of the significance of the French language, and of French ideas and values, throughout the world and in the US.

Designed to enhance awareness of the significance of the French language and Francophone culture in the US and globally, this book will be of interest to students and instructors across disciplines, from French language and culture to US history and international studies.

Kathleen Stein-Smith, *Chevalier dans l'Ordre des Palmes académiques*, is a dedicated foreign language educator and advocate. Her research, writing, and professional engagement are grounded in the role of French language and Francophone culture within the context of the significance of multilingualism in global citizenship. Since January 2015, she has served as the Chair of the American Association of Teachers of French (AATF) Commission on Advocacy.

The French in Our Lives
Past, Present, Future – Influence and Implications

Kathleen Stein-Smith

LONDON AND NEW YORK

First published 2022
by Routledge
4 Park Square, Milton Park, Abingdon, Oxon OX14 4RN

and by Routledge
605 Third Avenue, New York, NY 10158

Routledge is an imprint of the Taylor & Francis Group, an informa business

© 2022 Kathleen Stein-Smith

The right of Kathleen Stein-Smith to be identified as author of this work has been asserted in accordance with sections 77 and 78 of the Copyright, Designs and Patents Act 1988.

All rights reserved. No part of this book may be reprinted or reproduced or utilised in any form or by any electronic, mechanical, or other means, now known or hereafter invented, including photocopying and recording, or in any information storage or retrieval system, without permission in writing from the publishers.

Trademark notice: Product or corporate names may be trademarks or registered trademarks, and are used only for identification and explanation without intent to infringe.

British Library Cataloguing-in-Publication Data
A catalogue record for this book is available from the British Library

Library of Congress Cataloging-in-Publication Data
A catalog record has been requested for this book

ISBN: 978-0-367-90327-5 (hbk)
ISBN: 978-1-032-21969-1 (pbk)
ISBN: 978-1-003-02376-0 (ebk)

DOI: 10.4324/9781003023760

Typeset in Times New Roman
by codeMantra

Contents

	Introduction: The French Language in the World	1
1	The French-American Relationship: The Historical Context	13
2	The French-American Relationship in a Globalized World	19
3	French Language and Francophone Culture in the US Today	25
4	The Global Francophone Environment: Trends and Analysis	37
5	The Economic Impact of French as a Global and Local Business Language	49
6	Bilingualism: Benefits, Opportunities, and Analysis	57
7	French Language Learning in the US	68
8	The French Language and Francophone Culture in the US: French as a Heritage Language and Global Competency	75

Conclusions – The Future of French – The
French Language: Past, Present, and Future   87

Concluding Thoughts   102

References   105
Index   117

Introduction
The French Language in the World

French is a language of culture and diplomacy, of lifestyle and flair, and may be on its way to being the most widely spoken language in the world. Reflecting this worldwide trend of "soft power," appeal, and influence of French culture worldwide (Gray, 2017), French media and entertainment are enjoying unprecedented popularity in the US, with *Lupin*, *Dix pour cent*/Call My Agent, and other French TV series prominent in popular conversation (Solsman, 2021). However, this current resurgence of interest in French and Francophone culture through media and entertainment is just one example of a broader and deeper interest around the world, where we are all are flocking both to the *"Night of Ideas/Nuit des Idées"* and to the nearest *macaron* shop, while reading the latest Marc Levy novel, or listening to Québécoise singer Céline Dion at one of her frequent US or virtual appearances. French bilingualism is all around us – including a road trip to Québec, or an Air Canada flight, along with a visit to a French language event with friends, either face-to-face or virtually. Instead of *survivance*, *francoresponsabilité* and *francodurabilité* are in the air. To leverage this interest and *engagement*/commitment to French language and Francophone commitment, it is necessary to reexamine, rethink, and reimagine the role of French in our lives – past, present, and future.

French is everywhere – in our past and present, in the ideas of the Founding Fathers, and in our core values; in the names of our towns, cities, and other places, and in our family names; in the fine and performing arts and in the food, fashion, and entertainment we enjoy; and in the products, businesses, and organizations around us, as well as among our clients, customers, and employers. It is a language used around the world, useful for international business and in our own cultural lives. It is also the language of friends and neighbors, and even of our parents and grandparents. French is part of our lives – every day, and in every way – from our morning cronut or *beignet*, to the French stores and products in our local mall or main street; to Louisiana's *"Oui"* Initiative and French companies – like Engie that provides the very water we drink – and countless others that provide needed products and services, or employ us or our loved ones; and to an evening's entertainment of French film, television, or the arts – from the *Frères Lumière*, Monet, and the ballet to *Lupin*, and more.

Knowledge of the French language is an advantage and a privilege. A personal, professional, and cultural advantage and asset, it is also a privilege in that it provides an unparalleled window into the worldwide Francophone culture. While the French language fosters a fuller access to the great ideas, literature, and the arts that have been respected and admired for centuries, it also empowers us to more effectively connect with the global French-speaking or Francophone world in its diversity, and to our own French heritage and cultural identity in North America and in the US, where over 10M in the US claim French ancestry and where over 2M speak French at home (French-Americans, 2021; Ryan, 2013). More than 33M speak French in the Americas, and 300M speak French in the world, of whom well over 200M use French on a daily basis (Nadeau, 2021; OIF, 2018).

Any examination of the French language in the world includes consideration of its role in an increasingly multilingual world. Beyond French borders, most of those who speak French are bilingual or multilingual, also speaking one or more additional languages. Multilingualism transcends conversations among futurists – it is the norm in the globalized world. It is part of daily life, with more than half the world population speaking more than one language (Grosjean, 2010, 2020). French is a vibrant part of this global linguistic landscape, a global language spoken around the world, which generally exists within – and has adapted successfully to evolving within – multilingual environments. The online French dictionary, the *Dictionnaire des Francophones*, proposed by French President Macron in 2018 and launched in 2021, is noteworthy in that it has sought to include French words from outside France as a way of "bringing together and celebrating" the diversity of the world's French speakers (New French Dictionary, 2021). French is considered one of the most influential or powerful languages in the world, and has even been predicted to become the most widely spoken language in the world by mid-century (Chan, 2016; Gobry, 2014).

Notwithstanding the history of France and of the influence of France on the world of ideas, in the arts, and in history, French is a language of the future, with the number of French speakers growing rapidly, especially in Africa. In the US, French is a language of our history, from the earliest days of the European presence in what is now the US, and French ideas, military assistance, and political support were key to the successful outcome of the American Revolution (Shachtman, 2017). Yet again the French presence transcends history, and French is a language of today, spoken by over 2M in the US, where more than 10M claim French ancestry (French-Americans, 2021; Ryan, 2013). Most importantly, French is the language of the future, throughout the world, and here in the US, where new arrivals from France and from many points in the Francophone world are increasing the number of French speakers in many areas of the US and are increasing the vibrancy of the Francophone presence in the US, where a new generation of Francophones includes both Franco-Americans whose heritage may be measured in centuries as well as the newest Americans, and is characterized by diversity and global mindset (French Morning Staff, 2017).

This richness and complexity of the French factor in our lives is an advantage and a challenge – an advantage in that it is a common occurrence to hear French in towns and cities across the country, and in that online and streaming media have made French news, ideas, culture, and entertainment easily available everywhere. However, this very richness and complexity results in many separate Francophone communities and Francophone cultural identities, which is not in itself a disadvantage, but which may result in relative separation or isolation of many Francophone individuals and communities and lack of realization of the commonalities that exist in terms of a shared language and values (Putnam, 2000). In terms of the development of a sustainable Francophone community in the US, effective social and political action involves leveraging the collective influence of the entire community of French language speakers, supporters, and stakeholders as a broad-based coalition in a dynamic social movement to promote the sustainable development of the Francophone community in the US. The Francophone community is composed of French learners and teachers, Francophiles, Franco-Americans, and Americans of French heritage, as well as recent immigrants from France and the Francophone world along with their children and families, united by a shared purpose to strengthen and support the learning and use of French in our society.

In addition to being a language of culture and diplomacy, French is currently spoken around the world by 300 million people and is the official language of 35 governments. It is also the official language of the Olympic Games and an official language of numerous international organizations, including the United Nations. Of the 235 million who use French on a daily basis, 59% are located in Africa, which is also the area of fastest growth. Many daily speakers of French consider French an essential part of their educations and careers, and that it increases their ability to pursue higher education internationally in the French-speaking world. French is also considered to provide access to information (OIF, 2014, 2018; The Numbers, 2019).

With a population of 1.5 billion, or 16% of the world population and producing 16.5% of the world's wealth, and French as a common language fostering economic trade and cultural exchanges, the *Francophonie* or French-speaking world, is a major force. French is also a major media language, with news, information, and entertainment in French available throughout the world. It is also the fourth language on the internet. It is the fifth most widely spoken language in the world and the third most important language in international business. The number of French language speakers is projected to be 747 million by 2070. The *Organisation internationale de la Francophonie* (OIF), founded in 1970, has 88 members representing areas of the world where French is an official or widely spoken language (OIF, 2014, 2018).

French is also a language of education (Campus France, n.d.), and French students fall into two groups, those who learn French as a foreign language, and those for whom French is a medium of instruction. French is the language of education in over 30 countries or governmental jurisdictions, often in combination with one or more local mother tongue languages. French as a foreign language is taught around the world in schools and universities, as well as in language schools and centers, and through the *Alliance Française* and the *Institut Français*, learned by more than 50 million, making it the second most studied language in the world (OIF, 2014, 2018). French is a language of international education, both in terms of study abroad and in terms of access to education.

Beyond French borders, French is widely spoken in Europe, Asia, the Middle East, the Americas, and especially Africa. There are over 30 million French speakers in the Americas, with 11 million in the US alone, of whom over 2 million speak French at home (Ryan, 2013), found across the nation, but particularly in northern New England, Louisiana, New York, south Florida, and California. Their origins include many of French Canadian and Acadian descent as well as those from France and the expanse of the Francophone world.

French is often thought of as a global language with a local touch, used to share and to communicate within homes and communities around the world as well as in many international and global organizations and enterprises (Bourdillon, 2019). As with any language that has a presence in more than one culture, the language may vary from region to region, including local expressions, but it remains one language that unites Francophones *de sang et de coeur* around the world.

French as a Global and a Local Language – From Africa to the US

It is important for French language educators, supporters, and stakeholders communicate the importance of French as a global language rather than as a strictly European language. Most recently, the publication on the online *Dictionnaire de la langue française*. In addition, France is the second largest home for the production and consumption of hip-hop in the world (Meghelli, 2013).

While most Americans are well aware of iconic French symbols like the Eiffel Tower, relatively few of us may be aware of the French-language communities in Europe beyond French borders, and even fewer are aware of French around the world and in North America and the US. For those who believe in the significance of French as a global language, there are several takeaways from this. The first is that it is important for the French language partnership to work individually and in concert to increase awareness of the global nature of French, highlighting everything that France and French ideas have to offer, and also the global nature of French around the world and in local communities closer to home. Once this awareness has been established, and this may be more difficult than originally foreseen, it is equally important to follow up with systematic learning highlighting the role and use of French around the world and in local communities. Lastly, it is important to highlight and to demonstrate the role of French as a global language within the multilingual framework of global citizenship.

Challenges include the extent of this lack of awareness and its impact on the scope of the mission. These need to be addressed through education, training, and media. In terms of systematic learning, the lack of relevant materials and of a preexisting knowledge base on Francophone culture beyond French borders needs to be addressed through information sharing within professional and cultural organizations and in teacher training, with a second action step toward the development of relevant curricular materials. In terms of the role of French as a tool in making the world a better place through its role as a global language, US students and young Americans need to recognize both the importance of engaging proactively as global citizens and the importance of a specific skills set – or tools – such as multilingualism in effective global citizenship through both their education and the public conversation from the earliest age. It goes without saying that language learning, either through traditional foreign language education or through immersion, forms the foundation for effective use of additional languages in all areas of life, extending from the home to the global stage. The media plays a critical role in enabling and empowering widespread awareness as well as sustainable language learning and use. Creative media, including film, television, literature, and art, can inspire people of all ages to engage with a culture, an example of which is the unprecedented popularity of the TV series *Lupin*, among a global audience. Social media can engage many, including people of all ages and those unable to attend in-person events, in an additional culture and language. News media can bring different perspectives and worldviews within the reach of almost everyone.

Awareness of the global reach of French, knowledge of Francophone culture around the world and close to home, and engagement in global citizenship through multilingualism are cornerstones of advocacy and promotion of French language and Francophone culture in the US and beyond, and it is especially important for US students to learn more about Francophone Africa, Quebec, and Francophone Canada, and – especially – about our French and Francophone culture and the role of French in the US.

Moving forward, French language supporters need to continue to highlight all of the wonderful creativity and ideas of France and its culture, but just as importantly, we need to embrace the value of French as a language for the whole person – the intellectual, artist, and creative spirit, the foodie and fashionista, and for all of us who are passionate about our stories both individual and universal.

The greatest value of language is communication, and in addition to the importance of French language, French ideas, and Francophone culture themselves, it is also important to remember that France, its ideas, and its worldwide culture offer a pathway to understanding the diversity of the global world from a different perspective, as well as a model and example of the role of a global language in recognizing and cherishing cultural differences while bringing together diverse voices and perspectives both globally and locally.

Spanning the globe from Paris to Polynesia, the global Francophone culture includes global voices, while also being a truly American language, part of our US cultural identity. However, existing alongside the significance of French as a truly American language, with French language and ideas part of our story and identity, it is at least just as important for US students to have the experience of the struggle of learning another language in order to communicate in order to increase understanding of the struggle faced by so many in the world who leave their homeland for a variety of reasons in search of a new life. Beyond this individual experience of the language learner and the resulting development of empathy for others, language learning offers a window into another culture – in this case, the worldwide Francophone culture – and a means to communicate with others and to develop an understanding of different perspectives and worldviews.

Francophone Africa

While Americans are generally aware of the role of French within French borders and even in other European countries, relatively few think of French as a widely used language in Africa, and even fewer realize that well over half of French speakers are located in Africa where many countries and regions have French as an official or prevalent language, and where many international organizations use French as their official language. Most may be unaware that Kinshasa, in the République démocratique du Congo, and Abidjan are among the three largest French-speaking cities in the world, with Paris #2 and Montreal #4 (Hazan, 2016; World Bank, 2021).

While French is, of course, the language of France and its European neighbors Belgium, Switzerland, Luxembourg, and Monaco, the majority of French speakers are located outside of France and of Europe, with over half (59%) of French speakers located in Africa. Following current demographic trends, this growth is predicted to continue. In addition, sub-Saharan Africa and the Indian Ocean region account for 23%, and North Africa and the Middle East account for 45% of the 51M in the world who are learning French as a foreign language. Of the 81M students learning in French, within educational institutions where French is used as the medium of instruction rather than being taught solely as a school subject, 72.8% are located in Africa. In African nations, French is often ranked second, sometimes even ahead of local languages, and young people are tending to increasingly use French, with quality education in French a major factor in the future of French. Over 80% of Francophone parents in Africa and the Middle East wish to transmit the use of French to future generations. It is important to note that the French language is valued in education, the workplace, and business, and that it is not considered a purely intellectual pursuit (OIF, 2018).

As impactful as our lack of awareness and knowledge of French language and Francophone culture in Africa may be, a similar lack of awareness and knowledge of French language and Francophone culture close to home – in North America and in the US – is surprising, and cause for concern.

Québec and Francophone Canada

While we often consider the *rayonnement* of French language and Francophone culture from *l'Hexagone* to the rest of the world, we may not always consider the significance of French in Canada, our neighbor to the north. As Canada shares the longest land border with the US, millions in the US live in close proximity with a country where French is an official language, and many may be relatively unaware of this, familiar with popular culture icons Céline Dion and their favorite Canadian hockey teams, but relatively unaware of our shared history from the era of the earliest French explorers and *voyageurs*, of *La Nouvelle France*, and of French Canadian migration to the US at the time of the *Grand Dérangement* and of the migration of French Canadians to New England. Many Americans may not know the significance of June 24th as the Quebec national holiday or that the quintessentially California city of Los Angeles has had not one, but two, French-Canadian mayors (Pratte & Kay, 2016).

It is necessary to increase awareness of French language and Francophone culture in neighboring Canada through education, the media, and the public conversation. In terms of awareness, it is important to talk about Quebec and Francophone Canada in our families and to our students, and in our communities. In terms of education, it is important to develop both relevant curriculum and materials for both students and teachers in training. It is also important to point toward Francophone Canadian media, including information and news, entertainment and music, as well as literature and the arts.

It is equally important to remember that, although those in the US are more aware of French language and Francophone culture in Quebec, whether through the novels of Louise Penney or through the *Carnaval de Québec*, they may lack systematic and historical knowledge of Quebec and of Francophone Canada.

Still more interesting, and surprising, may be the lack of awareness and knowledge of French language and Francophone culture in the US, whether among Franco-Americans and Francophones of Maine and New England, those of French, Acadian, and Creole ancestry in Louisiana, or the many expats and immigrants and their families who live across the US.

Introduction: *French Language in the World* 9

As far as contemporary economic ties are concerned, Quebec and the US are close economic partners, with 20% of Quebec's GDP depending on exports to the United States and Quebec a major supplier of hydroelectric power to the US (CSIS, 2018; Noreau, 2017; US Dept. of State, 2021).

French Spoken in the US Today

In addition to the over 10M Americans of French ancestry, countless Francophiles, and the 1.3M and 176K students in the US learning French in K-12 and postsecondary education, respectively (American Councils, 2017; MLA, 2019), French is spoken by over 2M in the home in the US today (Ryan, 2013). Among those speaking French in the home, both heritage speakers and new arrivals from France and the Francophone world are included.

French speakers are numerous in many regions and large cities, from New York to San Francisco, and from Louisiana to New Hampshire and Maine, and French heritage can be found across the US, clearly illustrated by place names from Boise to Duluth, from Baton Rouge to Montpelier, and many more. French is the most frequently spoken language after English in several states, in Louisiana and Northern New England (Blatt, 2014). New York City has been mentioned as the unofficial Francophone capital of the US (Sicot & Brunet, 2020).

Maine and Louisiana are the states with the highest percentage of French speakers. In both states, the French language spoken includes both historical elements of the colonial era, as well as local elements, and in both Louisiana and Maine, a renaissance of French is underway (Fausset, 2015, 2019; Yechivi, 2021).

In Maine, the proximity of the border with Canada has resulted in a historical French presence, further reinforced by migration during the mid-19th to early-20th century of many French-Canadians, often to work in the textile mills. Traditionally, the Catholic Church played a significant role in supporting French, and the expression *qui perd sa langue, perd sa foi*, is well known within the context of *la survivance*. However, in the early 20th century, social and political factors, along with legislation limiting the teaching and use of French, resulted in language loss, and today efforts are underway to increase the learning and use of French in Maine. In Maine, French is still spoken, an exception in the US, where language loss has been the norm, by both Americans of French-Canadian descent and new arrivals from Francophone regions of Africa (Belluck, 2006; Fillak, 2018; McGuire, 2016).

French was brought to Louisiana by the French, the Acadians who were made to leave Canada during le Grand Derangement, and those who came to Louisiana from the Caribbean. In the early 20th century, legislation limiting the teaching and use resulted in language loss. However, in 1968 CODOFIL (Council for the Development of French in Louisiana) was created, and for more than 50 years has been working for the advancement of French language and Francophone culture in Louisiana through immersion programs and more. In 2018, Louisiana became the first US state to join the OIF, opening the door to additional cultural, commercial, and education opportunities for Francophones in Louisiana. In 2019, the first French Language Job Fair in New Orleans was held in collaboration with the French Consulate. Also in 2019, at the same time as the *Journée internationale de la Francophonie* (March 20th) CODOFIL launched the "Oui" Initiative, encouraging the use of French in local businesses and providing an online database of businesses with a French language presence (Cultural Services, 2019, 2021).

Creole, sometimes known as Kouri-Vini, developed from the interaction of French and African and Caribbean languages, is spoken by some 10,000 people, and is considered an endangered language (Louisiana Creole, 2021). In an initiative to encourage the next generation to reacquire the language of its cultural identity, Louisiana has been home to an increasing number of bilingual and immersion schools for the past 50 years (Carmosino, 2021; Louisiana French, 2021).

Florida is home to new arrivals from Haiti and African nations, as well as to French expats and numerous retirees from Quebec and the French-speaking world. It is important to include the fact that, within the total of 2M who speak French in the home in the US, includes those who speak French Creole. South Florida, home not only expats from France and other French-speaking countries around the world, is also home to a growing number of Haitians and has been considered the fastest growing French-speaking community in the US.

Conclusions

As a global language with a rich history across the disciplines, French offers an unparalleled window on both French culture and world culture, empowering those with French language skills to develop a worldview incorporating both global and interdisciplinary perspectives. Historically, a world language of communication and culture (Fumaroli, 2011), French is on the rise around the world, with more daily speakers and French language learners. It continues to be a leader in the world of ideas, demonstrated by the influence of its ideas ranging from those of

Introduction: French Language in the World 11

the Enlightenment/*siècle des Lumières* to the unprecedented popularity of the ideas of economist Thomas Piketty, and the 2019 Nobel Prize in Economics of Esther Duflo. Even the tragic 2019 damage to the Cathedral of Notre-Dame in Paris resulted in an outpouring of condolences and support from around the world, including the donation in 2021 of the proceeds from a book about the fire by world-famous author Ken Follett for the restoration of a Breton cathedral (Willsher, 2021).

Within the context of 21st-century skills, the French language is certainly represented as one of the most important and influential languages in the world. The current campaign for French was launched by French President Emmanuel Macron in 2018 based on the role and value of French as a language of education and learning, of communication, and of creativity (France Diplomacy, International Strategy, 2019; Macron to Turn Derelict Chateau, 2018) is within the framework of 21st-century skills, by virtue of its role in multilingualism as a global competency and by the 21st-century skills set commonly referred to as the 4Cs – critical thinking, communication, collaboration, and creativity.

While the learning and use of French are evolving differently in each region, these concepts of learning, communication, and creativity can be found in the initiatives both global and local, of the *Alliance Française and Institut Français*, and of the OIF. Examples in the Americas and specifically in the US include the *Centre de la Francophonie des Amériques* (CFA), the CODOFIL, and the Franco-American Centre of New Hampshire (FACNH). The campaign for French is accompanied and supported by local campaigns and initiatives within educational organizations and institutions including the American Association of Teachers of French (AATF) National French Week and many others. Community and heritage groups play an essential role in sustaining interest and engagement through initiatives including the *French Canadian Legacy Podcast and Blog* and *New Hampshire PoutineFest* among others. Franco-American authors and artists, including David Vermette, Robert B. Perreault, Josée Vachon, and Zachary Richard, and the musical groups Sweet Crude, Le Vent du Nord, and many more, play an essential role.

It is perhaps the role of creativity – of appreciation of the arts and of the creative act itself – that is the least frequently mentioned. However, it may be the most important in terms of developing sustainable interest and engagement in the language and its culture. This is a true area of strength for the promotion of French based on its appeal across the centuries and across the arts. Most recently, technology has become increasingly important in the diffusion, consumption, and enjoyment of culture, and the appeal of French has been highlighted by the unprecedented popularity of French and French-themed media offerings like

Lupin and *Call My Agent*, both inspired by traditional areas of strength, French literature, and the French cinema, which are clear indications of the resurgence of French in the US and around the world, not to mention the popularity of French books translated into English, and of movies based on French books or remakes of French films.

The value of French language skills and knowledge of Francophone culture lies in its ability to foster connections not only to Francophone cultures around the world but also to our own cultural identity past, present, and future. In addition, in a globalized world, multilingualism is part of the 21st-century skills set, with French a global language. The challenge is to rebuild US French language skills and interest in France and Francophone cultures among Americans. This can best be accomplished through language learning – increasing the availability of French language learning opportunities in our educational institutions and in our communities, taking advantage of all that technology and online learning have to offer, and in bringing the intrinsic appeal of the language and culture to our communities and to our society as a whole, again leveraging the power of technology in support of French language communications, media, and creativity for all.

The use of French needs to be part of our daily lives – the time for resolutions and good intentions has passed; French needs to become a habit, part of the fabric of our regular routine, used automatically in a wide range of situations and settings (Guthridge, 2017; Roberts, 2019). The time to act is now, and the situation is urgent (Kotter, 2008), further exacerbated by the COVID-19 pandemic. With heritage language communities constantly evolving and facing language loss, and the availability of foreign languages – including French – decreasing in our schools and colleges, there is a real risk that the use of French in the US may soon be limited to a relatively small number of new Americans and to dedicated heritage speakers and Francophiles.

In order to prevent French language loss, a broad coalition of French language stakeholders, including parents and communities, educators, business and government, Francophiles in all walks of life, with external partners such as France and Québec, needs to act together with the shared goal of increased learning and use of French – using public relations and marketing, advocacy, and political and social action to achieve these goals.

Action steps include working to strengthen French language learning opportunities for all, and creating a vibrant French-language social and media presence so that *la langue de Molière* will continue to be heard on the streets of our cities and towns. French is, however, a global and a local language.

1 The French-American Relationship
The Historical Context

From the visits of the Founding Fathers to Versailles (Kisluk-Grosheide & Rondot, 2018) to plead the cause of the colonies during the American Revolution to the widespread fascination with *Emily in Paris* and the experiences of "Frenchfluencers" (Meltzer, 2020) – Americans who blog and/or post about their experiences from France – the French-American relationship has been both enduring and multifaceted (USDOS, 2020). While the French language and Francophone culture in the US represent not only France but also additional countries of origin in Europe, Africa, and beyond, it is important to recognize the pivotal role of France not only in the history and culture of the global *Francophonie* but also in both US history and culture.

Founded on the ideals of the *siècle des Lumières,* or French Enlightenment, and with France as our ally in the American Revolution, the US has had a long-standing relationship that predates even its very existence (France Diplomacy, France and the United States, (2021)). From the earliest European explorers and settlers to the present day, the conversation between our two cultures has been ongoing. France was the first ally of the new nation, welcoming the Founding Fathers to Paris and to Versailles, and supporting the revolutionary cause, and France has been an ally of the US during both world wars. The French and American people are equally linked. Throughout our history, Americans have flocked to France, Paris, and the Louvre, and American writers and artists have found inspiration and a second home in Paris (McCullough, 2011; Spring, 2017). Even our language, although Germanic, has been greatly influenced by French throughout history.

Whether taking a walk through most cities and towns in the US, or a stroll through history, it is impossible to miss the numerous references to France and to the French impact on the US and on Americans throughout our history, with examples including our nation's capital, designed by Pierre L'Enfant, and Central Park in New York City,

DOI: 10.4324/9781003023760-2

reflecting the image of French parks and gardens (Ives, 2018). From a glass of champagne to celebrate a special occasion or a *macaron* nibbled while walking down a crowded downtown avenue or a quiet small-town street, to weighty tomes written on the impact of France and of French ideas on American culture and on Americans, French is everywhere – including items like "French" fries and "French" dressing, whose ties to France are doubtful at best (Thiery, 2021). Our popular culture is filled with references to France and to French ideas, French style, French cinema, French cuisine, French technology, and to Francophone culture around the world. From French films in the parks of New York City to French period rooms in the Metropolitan Museum of Art, and from French TV series online to high-profile museum exhibits and appearances, French culture is everywhere. In addition, French cuisine, from the "cronut" to the newest French restaurant, is as popular as ever among Americans. Lastly, the enduring attraction of France, and of all things French, for Americans, has drawn writers, artists, and tourists to France, and especially to Paris, since the Founding Fathers pleaded the American Revolutionary cause in Paris. It is difficult not to be aware of the French in our lives, even if we do not speak a word of French, and even if we have not – yet – visited France. In addition, as French has been an American language since the earliest French explorers and settlers, a trip across the US may also include the Franco Route in New England, Coeur d'Alene and Boise, Idaho, or Lafayette, Louisiana, as French place names are found throughout the country, and the state motto of Minnesota is *l'Étoile du Nord*.

As a global language, French is spoken by 300M around the world, with over half of those who speak French on a daily basis in Africa. French is the language spoken by 33M in the Americas, and in the home of 2M in the US (Nadeau, 2021; OIF, 2018; Ryan, 2013) – not only descendants of early French settlers and French Canadians but also by recent arrivals from France, Africa, Haiti, and the global Francophonie.

Our Shared French History

While we often think of our British heritage, French explorers, colonists, and other stakeholders were actively present in what is now the US, parts of which have also been known as *Nouvelle France*. Interestingly, the prevalent US cultural narrative, written primarily in English, has offered an interpretation of our US history and culture viewed primarily through a British English-language lens or perspective despite the fact that even a quick glance at a modern map of the US reveals countless French place names.

From the explorations of Jacques Cartier and Samuel de Champlain, French place names highlight the historical French presence in the US from New Orleans to Vermont (Fischer, 2008). Even today, place names like Detroit, St. Louis, and Maine witness the French presence in North America and in the US. For example, since French explorers often served as guides for other settlers after the US purchased the Louisiana Territory, French words were used to describe many aspects of the frontier experience, such as *portage, rapids,* and *bayou.* In addition to French place names, French family names are frequent in the US, reflecting the French presence in the US beyond that of exploration, explorers, and place names. Our American Revolution was framed by the ideas of the French Enlightenment, or *siècle des Lumières,* and the Marquis de Lafayette was perhaps the best known of the French supporters of the American Revolution. French Canadians were also among those who rallied to the cause and fought for our independence in the Green Mountain Boys of Vermont.

French is one of the most frequently spoken languages in the US, with French spoken by more than 2M in the home and the most widely spoken language, after English, in four states – Maine, Vermont, New Hampshire, and Louisiana. It is the most widely spoken language in the US, after French and Spanish, and the most widely spoken language after English and Spanish in an additional eight states, making French a widely spoken language in nearly a quarter of our 50 states (Blatt, 2014). Over 10M Americans claim French ancestry, including over a million French Canadians who migrated to New England, where they played a vital role in the industrialization of the region. Prudent Beaudry, originally from Québec, served as Mayor of Los Angeles (Pratte & Kay, 2016). Other famous Franco-Americans include Jack Kerouac, Grace Metalious, Warren Buffett, Paul Revere, and Henry David Thoreau.

French as an American Language

Not only is French one of the most frequently spoken languages in the US, but our relationship with French is one of the oldest, dating from well before the US even existed. With over 10M Americans of French heritage, the French language – spoken by more than 2M Americans at home – is part of the ongoing American story from the earliest arrivals of European explorers until today's most recent arrivals from France and the Francophone world.

While the term Franco-American is generally used to describe the descendants of the million French Canadians who came to New England during the period from the mid-19th century to the early decades of the 20th century, Americans of French heritage include descendants of the early explorers, French often referred to as Huguenots who came to the US for religious reasons, French Canadians and French who fought alongside the Americans during the American Revolution, French who fled the French Revolution, as well as *Acadiens* victims of the *Grand Dérangement*, the deportations of Acadians from what are now New Brunswick and the Maritime provinces, after the fall of *Nouvelle France*. In fact, the founding of Mobile, Alabama, predates that of New Orleans. The best-known part of this ongoing relationship is perhaps the exile of the Acadians, made famous by Longfellow in his *Evangeline*, and the American term "cajun" comes from the French word *acadien*. In addition, the US has been home to Haitian populations throughout our history, along with other groups from the Francophone world and, of course, France.

A large part of what is now the US was once part of the French colonial empire in North America, and the loss of the North American colonies was part of an ongoing wider conflict between France and England. Among the results of the loss of *Nouvelle France* is the fact that our US story has focused on the relatively short period during which the original 13 states were British colonies, rather than on the actually more extensive period and geographic area that much of the new nation had been under French influence, and on our British heritage, rather than on the role of the ideas of the *siècle des Lumières*, or Enlightenment, clearly seen in our Declaration of Independence and rather than on the roles of the Marquis de Lafayette, Rochambeau, and others in the Revolution (Shachtman, 2017). In fact, little mention is made of the fact that many of the Founding Fathers – Jefferson, Franklin, and others – actually spoke French and travelled to France to seek support for the revolution, and that Lafayette returned later in life for a triumphal tour of the US (Unger, 2002).

Moreover, the interest in French ideas and culture – far from waning after the American Revolution – kept increasing, as American writers including Henry James, found inspiration in France, and American artists and art lovers thronged to the newly created Louvre museum throughout the 19th and into the 20th century (McCullough, 2011). At present, the number of French living in the US is increasing, with new arrivals each year, in addition to new arrivals from around the Francophone world.

While the role and importance of French language and Francophone culture in the US is significant, it remains often understated, or absent altogether, from the US history we learn in school, and in our media and public conversation. We tend to not venture beyond a few mentions of the earliest years and the American Revolutionary War period, and generally do not discuss the subsequent role of the French and Francophone presence in our history and culture. French is indeed part of our US history and cultural identity – past, present, and future.

The Role of French and Francophone Culture in US Cultural Identity

Not surprisingly, the most interesting parts of the French and American story are, by far, the enduring relationship between the French and American peoples, and between French and Francophone culture and our US cultural identity. It would be difficult to imagine a library, museum, or other cultural venue where French ideas and creativity did not play an influential role. American museums hold significant collections of French art, and numerous American writers have featured French settings and characters in classic American works.

American celebrities, including Jodie Foster and Bradley Cooper, speak French, as do public figures John Kerry, Mitt Romney, and Antony Blinken. French ideas have fascinated Americans, including the writings of Sanche de Gramont (who actually became an American), Jean-Jacques Servan Schreiber, and Thomas Piketty. Worldwide best-selling French novelist Marc Levy, whose characters transcend French and US stereotypes, has made his home in the US. Famous American writers who lived in Paris include Gertrude Stein, Ernest Hemingway, and F. Scott Fitzgerald. Contemporary "Frenchfluencers," including David Lebovitz and Lindsey Tramuta, write, blog, and post to social media from Paris. Julia Child, MFK Fisher, and Richard Olney are among the many Americans culinary figures influenced by French cuisine, not to mention French culinary celebrities in the US, who include Jacques Pepin, Daniel Boulud, and Jacques Torres. American artists Josephine Baker, Mary Cassat, and John Taylor Sargent are among the American artists who made Paris home. Among the many American films portraying France, *Midnight in Paris*, *Before Sunset*, and *Charade* are just a few of the best known. American writers including Cara Black, Diane Johnson, and Elaine Sciolino have made their home in or spend portions of the year in Paris, while former French Ambassador to the US, Gérard Araud, made his home in New

York after his service. 20th-century French-American love stories include Yves Montand and Marilyn Monroe, and Juliette Greco and Miles Davis (Thiery, 2020b). Americans have also fought in France in both World Wars, and most recently, numerous Americans have been among those who have donated to the restoration fund for the Cathedral of Notre-Dame.

Conclusions

The French reality in America is undeniable, including our history and story from the earliest days of European exploration, and there has been a constant French and Francophone presence in what is now the US, to varying degrees, throughout our history. However, as much of our history has been told through a British lens, reflecting only the final years of our colonial history, a priority should be developing books and other media and information highlighting the French contribution.

Exposure to the ideas, the arts, and lifestyle, always present both at home and through travel, has been intensified by recent advances in telecommunications and media, and – with interruption caused by the COVID-19 pandemic – by relative ease and accessibility of travel and study abroad. The role of French schools in the US is supplemented by the study of French in schools and colleges and through dual-language immersion programs. However, the most frequently overlooked factor in the conversation about the French reality in America is the presence of over 10M Americans of French heritage, who have kept the language alive and the culture vibrant for centuries. In addition, in recent years, an increasing number of French and other Francophone nationals are making their home in the US, providing a steady stream of new mother-tongue speakers to Francophone communities (Thiery, 2020a) throughout the country.

While the French presence, past and present, is clearly demonstrated, the future of French appears even more promising, as more and more Americans routinely access French and Francophone media for information and entertainment, and are using French on a regular basis in their homes, in the workplace, and in their communities.

2 The French-American Relationship in a Globalized World

Introduction

The traditional relationship between France and the US has been transformed by globalization and by the interconnectedness of the globalized world, as have the relationships between the French and the Americans, as well as the relationship between Americans and the Francophone world. The historical relationship between France and the US, from the earliest days of the European exploration of North America, has been broadened and transformed by the impact of globalization, with the role of both French and English as global languages and the "soft power" of France, which includes both its influence and the worldwide appeal of its ideas, culture, and lifestyle (Gray, 2017). French language skills, facilitating access to French media and entertainment, support development of a more cosmopolitan or global mindset.

Rather than the more one-on-one relationship between France and the US that had historically existed, both France and the US today play a global role both in the complex and constantly changing realm of international relations around the world as well as within multilateral efforts to effectively address complex global issues ranging from the environment and climate change to global health (FocusEconomics, 2020; Gordon & Meunier, 2001, 2002). It is interesting to note that two recent US Secretaries of State, John Kerry and Antony Blinken, have been fluent in French.

In terms of political relations, France and the US are allies and cooperate in many areas, with ceremonies and official visits by officials on both sides commemorating this alliance. France enjoys a positive image in the US, with an 87% approval rating in a recent Gallup poll (Saad, 2016). There is a French caucus in the US Congress, along with similar groups in the French National Assembly and Senate. It is

DOI: 10.4324/9781003023760-3

estimated that 300K French nationals live in North America (France Diplomacy, France and the US, 2019). In terms of economic relations, trade between France and the US is 140B, France is a major trading partner of the US, and the US is the top destination for French investment, and the US is the top foreign investor in France. American investment in France is increasing, and French companies employ nearly 750K in the US, and US companies employ 500K in France (French Treasury, 2017, 2019; Thiery, 2018).

The significant cultural, scientific, and academic cooperation includes exchanges and joint projects. Mutual interest on the part of both French and Americans is another important factor, and over 600K French visit the US, and over 4M Americans visit France in a typical year. 450 French books have been translated into English in the most recent year (Cultural Services, 2021a), and Americans and French share interest in books, movies, and TV from both cultures.

The French–American Relationship

The French–American relationship can be viewed through the lens of history, culture, or business and economics. It is interesting to reflect on the trajectory of the French–American relationship over the course of the relatively short history of the US. Beginning with the early French presence in North America and in what is now the US through French support for the American cause in the American Revolution, through the role of France and French culture in American culture from the earliest visits of Americans to the Louvre to the numerous artists and writers who made Paris their home through the 19th century and beyond, the admiration held by Americans for France and French culture was widespread. In the 20th century, the French and the Americans were allies in both world wars.

However, since that time, the relationship between France and the US, and at times between the French and American people, for a variety of reasons including globalization, has become more complex in its political, economic, and cultural aspects. In terms of the French–American relationship, globalization has been described in terms of foreign investment in and earnings abroad by French multinationals (MNCs), French leadership on global and international issues, and the influence of American ideas on many aspects of French life, including the presence of McDonald's in France to the role of consultants in the French government. This question of French and Americans in the globalized world has even been featured in films including *The French Minister/Quai d'Orsay* and *Two Days in Paris*.

French ideas of the Enlightenment formed the foundation of both the American Revolution and the new republic, with Founding Father visits to both Paris and Versailles. In addition, French military support and assistance during the American Revolution played a major role in the outcome, with Lafayette, de Rochambeau, and de Grasse among the most widely known (Shachtman, 2017). The influence of French ideas and humanist values as a cornerstone of our own has continued, and on a cultural, social, and intellectual level, the exchange of ideas between France and the US has never been stronger. These ideas, which launched the French Revolution, have had an influence not only in France and in the US but also in Europe and around the world.

International influence, however, includes both American influence and French influence. In terms of political relations on the global stage, France and the US are both members of NATO and the G8, and numerous international organizations. France plays an active role at the UN in virtually all areas. Both France and the US are permanent members of the Security Council of the United Nations, and French and English are the permanent languages of the International Olympic Committee. France exerts major influence and leadership in global health and global health security, with a tradition of prioritizing universal healthcare at home and around the world.

In an interesting example of French influence in the US, in 2018, the US state of Louisiana joined the *Organisation internationale de la Francophonie* (Louisiana Joins, 2018). In terms of economic relations, the US is the largest foreign investor in France, and the US is one of the most important destinations for French foreign investment. The US and France are major trading partners, with commercial transactions averaging over $1B per day (France Country Commercial Guide, 2019). Both France and the US are actively engaged in all the world's regions – South America and the Caribbean, Africa, the Middle East, Asia, and the Pacific Rim – with France exercising more influence in areas that have been associated with France in the past.

The influence and impact of France on the US and on the world stem from the prestige and the global reach of its ideas, culture, and language throughout the world for historical, economic, and political reasons, but also – most importantly – due to the appeal and attractiveness of France and French thought worldwide, reflected in the number of visitors (approaching 90M) to France annually and through its presence among the nations with the most "soft power," or influence, in the world (Gray, 2017). Part of this soft power reflects the power of French brands, ranging from fashion, beauty, and culinary global brand names like Dior, l'Oréal, and la Veuve Cliquot (Cooke, 2021), to global names in technology and environmental services like Airbus and Suez/Engie, to the world-famous Louvre museum, considered by many to be the best-known art museum in the world, lending its name to institutions in the UAE and soon in Shanghai, and serving as the setting of a Beyonce and Jay-Z video (Chrisafis, 2019).

However, in the digital world, the intentional use of online and social media, in addition to more traditional forms of education and communication, is part of a millennial strategy to extend and maintain influence. Building on historical, cultural, and educational institutions and networks like the Sorbonne, as well as the worldwide presence of the *Institut Français,* and *the Alliance Française,* the ability of France to communicate not only the big ideas like climate change that are likely to resonate with people around the world of all ages, but perhaps especially with the young, as well as the appeal of French lifestyle, through the digital media readily accessible to a larger and larger number, plays a role in its growing and sustainable global influence and soft power.

Beyond politics, business, and media, the French–American relationship rests with individuals, and there is a remarkable level of activity concerning France, the French language, and Francophone culture in the US stemming from the popularity of the French language and culture among US students and Francophiles of all ages, the historical French presence, including over 10M Americans of French heritage, in large portions of the US, and significant numbers of French expats and recent arrivals to the US from around the Francophone world. In addition to Franco-Americans and Americans of French ancestry from around the world, a significant number of French nationals make the US and North America their home. Over 5M Americans visit France each year, and nearly 2M French visit the US (France Diplomacy, Tourism, 2021; Statista, 2021). France is one of the top destinations for US students who study abroad, and an increasing number of French students study in the US (Campus France, n.d.; IIE, 2020). French is the second most popular language studied in the US at both the K-12 and postsecondary levels (American Councils, 2017), and over 500 French books are translated into English in the US each year (Cultural Services, 2021a). However, while 39% of the French speak English (EC, 2012), only 12% of US students study French in school (American Councils, 2017; French Americans, 2021).

It is interesting to note the enduring interest among French and Americans for the language and culture of the other – through language learning, television, film, and media, books in translation, and publications like the bilingual *France-Amérique,* founded during

World War II by the French in New York City, and offering "a compilation of portraits, reports, essays, and interviews to inspire thought and debate" (France-Amérique).

Additionally, there are many organizations and institutions that are dedicated to the French–American relationship. For example, the French Cultural Foundation,

> honoring the past, celebrating the present, and building for the future, is composed of individuals and organizations committed to advancing and enhancing partnerships between France and America. Our programs highlight our shared culture, and a way of life that emphasizes *independence*, *creativity*, and *excellence*.
> (French Cultural Foundation)

The French–American Foundation, "Advancing dialogue between French & American Leaders," has as its mission "to perpetuate more than two centuries of shared ideals and friendship; to build lasting, practical working ties; and to advance solutions to problems of shared concern." Secretary of State Antony Blinken is a 1998 FAF Young Leader (French–American Foundation).

Conclusions

The relationship between France and the US has evolved in response to globalization and the interconnectedness of the globalized world. Rather than the traditional one-on-one relationship that existed between the young nation and France, its earliest ally, the French–American relationship exists in a globalized and multilateral world, with France and the US, along with their languages, playing significant roles in an evolving world on a wide range of issues. While the traditional friendship has remained strong, with close political ties, economic partnerships and cooperation, scientific, academic, and cultural collaborations and exchanges, and mutual interest in each other's culture, the relationship has evolved into one of collaboration and cooperation grounded in our shared history. From the early French explorers and the era of New France, to the role of France in the American Revolution and the design of the nation's capital by Pierre L'Enfant, to recent state visits by Presidents Sarkozy, Hollande, and Macron, along with the founding of the bipartisan French Caucus in the US Congress, the relationship between France and the US has evolved into a mature global relationship of two old friends, reflecting both strong ties and individual differences. The resurgence of interest in French media, including the phenomenal success of the TV series *Lupin*, among Americans, and the response among Americans to the tragic Cathedral of Notre-Dame fire, only serve to confirm the strength of the French–American relationship – past, present, and future. In order to sustain the historical relationship between the Americans and the French, it is essential for us to continue to learn about each other – through an interdisciplinary approach and using all of today's technologies to access information, education, and entertainment. However, our past informs our present, and it is important not to base our understanding of French and Francophone culture solely on entertainment, or through movies and fiction, but also through the lenses of nonfiction reading and media and interdisciplinary learning. Our present understanding of the French, and of the French–American story, is enriched by an understanding of our past, and an understanding of people and events like the return visit made by the Marquis de Lafayette to the US years after the Revolution and the accounts of the early *voyageurs* play as important a role as the observations of contemporary observers including Bernard-Henri Lévy, "Frenchfluencers," and others. In order to build a valid understanding of the French–American relationship, a multiplicity of viewpoints and perspectives is essential. Just as our shared history and a variety of information sources are essential in building true understanding and appreciation of the French–American relationship, so too our understanding of the French–American relationship in a globalized world is based on our past and present, and on a multiplicity of information sources from throughout the Francophone world.

3 French Language and Francophone Culture in the US Today

Introduction

While the French language and Francophone culture have always been part of American life, this is perhaps even more true today than ever before because of the interconnectedness of the globalized world. In addition to French place names throughout the country, the role of France and of French ideas in the American Revolution, and the long-standing relationship between France and the US and between the French and the Americans, the ease of travel and additional means of communication have made access to authentic French information, education, media, and entertainment exponentially more available to the average American. Rather than having to search out a newsstand to buy a possibly outdated and expensive copy of a French magazine or newspaper as was the norm in the not-too-distant past, or to search out a bookstore or movie theater specializing in French language books and movies, all of these things and more are readily available through a laptop, tablet, or phone. Alongside Americans of French ancestry, who number more than 10M, an increasing number of French nationals and new Americans from around the Francophone world are making their home in the US, with New York City alone home to more than 80,000 Francophones (Sicot & Brunet, 2020), are adding to the vibrancy of the French language and Francophone culture across the country. Beyond US borders, the French and Francophone presence throughout the Americas – including Canada, Saint Pierre and Miquelon, the Caribbean, and Latin America, bringing the number of those who speak French in the Americas to more than 33M (Nadeau, 2021) – plays an important role in the US. While sometimes referred to as a "foreign" language in the US, French is an American language and has been so since the beginning of the European era in the Americas, spoken over large areas of what is now the US as well as in the

DOI: 10.4324/9781003023760-4

Caribbean and Latin America, and many US towns and cities are home to vibrant Francophone communities. Francophone culture is equally present in the US, treasured by Francophones, Francophiles, and Americans of French heritage, and various aspects are the object of interest and study by many, ranging from historians, artists, and literary scholars to foodies, "fashionistas," movie lovers and travelers. French cultural events, cuisine, and entertainment are readily available throughout the US, as are French books, media, and news (Bulgur, 2021). French architecture is prominent in many cities, most notably in the nation's capital, designed by Pierre L'Enfant, and in New York City, home to the Statue of Liberty, the most famous gift to the US by France. Many American celebrities and public figures speak French, many US students study abroad in France, and "Frenchfluencers," Americans who live in and blog or post from France, play a significant role in social media (Meltzer, 2020). In addition to the US proper, French language and Francophone cultures is close at hand beyond our borders, in Québec and Canada, Saint Pierre and Miquelon, and in the Caribbean. In the US, there are well over 10M Americans of French heritage, French is spoken at home by more than 2M in the US, and widely spoken in 11 of our US states. French has long been, and continues to be, the second most widely studied language in the US. Dual language immersion programs and French heritage language programs are creating a new generation of bilingual French-speaking Americans (Carmosino, 2021). It is important to remember that today's Franco-Americans and Francophones have diverse origins and stories, ranging from descendants of the earliest French explorers and settlers, through the deportation of many Acadians to Louisiana and other regions, and the ongoing migration from Québec into New England and beyond, to more recent arrivals from France, Francophone Africa, and beyond.

French Language and Francophone Culture in the US

A simple walk through a US mall is replete with examples of French culture – from Izod and Jacadi, to Sandro and Maje, and more, and one of the primary access points to New York City is the Verrazzano Narrows Bridge, named for Giovanni de Verrazzano, who sailed for the New World from the French port of Rouen (Sciolino, 2020). The influence of the French language and Francophone culture in the US is partly due to the presence of France, along with its language and culture, in what is now the US since before our country existed, but is also part of the global effect of French soft power, or the ability

French Language and Francophone Culture 27

to influence and to persuade, around the world. France's rise in 2017 and 2019 as the top global soft power only confirms its attractiveness and its ability to influence and persuade around the world, as well as here in the US (Gray, 2017). For these reasons and more, despite a relatively lower number of mother tongue speakers, and because of its prestige in international diplomacy, French remains one of the most powerful languages in the world (Chan, 2016). An earlier study even suggests that – by mid-21st century – French could be the most widely spoken language in the world (Gobry, 2014). French is indeed a global language, and predictions increase its continued increase in importance due to a variety of factors, including it exponential growth in Africa.

The relationship between France and the US, and perhaps most importantly, between the French and the Americans, has endured for centuries. This relationship between a venerable deeply rooted culture and a new republic may be both surprising and very real. Americans have always been interested in France, from the earliest days of *la Nouvelle France*, and French support of our American Revolution through the widespread interest in all things French among American Francophiles, artists, writers, and performing artists throughout our history. France has been both a physical and spiritual destination and homeland for so many, from our Founding Fathers to the present day. France and the French are also interested in the US. From the earliest explorers and French support of the American Revolution to today's expats, start-ups, multinational corporations, and direct investment, France and the French have always been interested and engaged in the American experience –now, perhaps, more than ever before.

At the present time, over 2M in the US speak French in the home, numerous exchange and dual-language immersion programs exist, and French is the second most popular foreign language in the US. In addition, France is among the most popular destinations for US tourists abroad and for US students studying abroad. On the other hand, the US is the top destination for French international tourists and for French students studying abroad beyond Europe.

The question really is how best to leverage this mutual interest – Why and how should we take advantage and maximize the French interest in our country to advance language learning and actual intercultural understanding. Many US cities have a French "feel" due to the influence of French architecture and design, and countless Americans live within a relatively short distance of Montréal and Québec City, not to mention many more who visit fictional depictions of these French influences in Epcot and Las Vegas. Along with so many around the world, Americans enjoy and appreciate French film, food, fashion, fiction, and more. While perhaps not as readily visible, many French technology products and services, including banking, financial services, tires, and energy and environmental services are popular in the US – with examples including BNP, Société Générale, AXA, Michelin, and Suez/Engie. In addition, French start-ups have proliferated in recent years, and the automobile maker Peugeot is planning a return to the US. The interest in – and appreciation of – French lifestyle and culture on the one hand, and of its technology on the other, drive the increasing interest in travel, study abroad, and learning the language. Fortunately, the French government, through its cultural diplomacy, facilitates exposure to French film, theatre, musical performances, and art, as well as cultural exchanges (FACE).

The French and the Americans

It is interesting to consider the reasons why Franco-Americans may have been relatively unnoticed, and even invisible, in our US history, and these reasons may include the "melting pot" metaphor of American identity and resulting assimilation, or even the fact that so many Franco-Americans came from nearby Québec rather than from faraway homelands.

However, the truth remains that, although more numerous than many other groups, Franco-Americans – and by extension, the French in the US – have been largely overlooked (Vermette, 2016). As the French and Francophone presence in the US has been so invisible and overlooked, a logical question would be as to where this French presence actually is. While the Franco-American population may be largely situated in the Northeast, the French and Francophone presence can be found across the country, including – first and foremost – New England and Louisiana, but extending throughout the country as evidenced not only by place names like St. Louis and Boise but also through the existence of French speakers in places like Missouri and Illinois, and the fact that Los Angeles has actually had two French-Canadian mayors.

As for the present, the fastest-growing Francophone community is said to be in South Florida, where French Creole is spoken by large numbers in the Haitian community (Blatt, 2014). The French nationals living in the US is increasing, and significant numbers of French expats live in cities like New York, Boston, Miami, and San Francisco. While French is prominent in global media, it is also on the airwaves across the US.

French Experiences in the US Today

France has played an important role in the development of American civilization, from the revolutionary period through centuries as a destination for American artists and thinkers. However, the French experience transcends the historical to become part of our daily lives today. Those who want to eat French food, wear French fashions, and send their children to French schools can do so in most large US cities and many smaller ones.

In the US, in addition to schools that follow the French curriculum, there are immersion programs in US public and charter schools, along with French heritage language programs. In New York City alone, from the shopping and eateries in Le District, one can experience French culture and ambience at Albertine, the French Institute *Alliance Française*, the *Maison Française* at Columbia University or NYU, the Metropolitan Museum of Art, the Conservatory Garden in Central Park, Greenwich Village and its Washington Square Park arch, and numerous restaurants, cafés, and stores throughout the city.

Not only was the nation's capital designed by a Frenchman, Pierre L'Enfant, but its enduring low-profile skyline and green spaces maintain an Old World feeling, and the National Gallery of Art houses a wonderful collection of French Impressionist art. There are also numerous events at the French Embassy's *Maison Française*. In Philadelphia, not only was the City Hall designed by a Frenchman, one can also visit significant collections of French art in the city's museums. In New Orleans and the surrounding Cajun country, the architecture, cuisine, and beignets at the Café du Monde reflect both history and current life. There is a whole generation of new Francophones in Louisiana, thanks to 50+ years of CODOFIL and French language immersion. In keeping with its historic name, in Montpelier, the general atmosphere is reminiscent of a French country town. French heritage and ambience can be found throughout the Midwest, through art, food, and history, and the town of Gallipolis, Ohio, was founded by French who came to the US in the aftermath of the French Revolution.

Moreover, there are Bastille Day celebrations in over 200 locations across the country, and Québec's Montreal, Québec City, French islands Saint Pierre and Miquelon, Martinique, Guadeloupe, and Saint-Martin, and countless wonderful Francophone destinations are just a short trip from the US.

Famous Americans Who Speak French

Famous Americans who speak French include both present-day celebrities as well as historical figures. Contemporary celebrities and famous Americans who speak French include Bradley Cooper, Jodie Foster, John Kerry, Mitt Romney, Kevin Kline, Jane Fonda, John Malkovich, Joseph Gordon-Levitt, Angela Davis, sports celebrities like Serena Williams, Tony Parker (American father, born in Belgium, and played in France before his US career), and many more (Tony Parker, 2021).

Historical figures include Founding Fathers Benjamin Franklin and Thomas Jefferson, as well as Jacqueline Kennedy, along with authors like Jack Kerouac. Financier Felix Rohatyn, who saved New York from bankruptcy in the 1970s, though born in Austria, came to the US from France, spoke French, worked at the famous Lazard Frères and later served as US ambassador to France. Secretary of State Antony Blinken, who lived in France as a child and teen, is fluent in French.

In 1989, to celebrate the bicentennial of the French Revolution, American soprano Jessye Norman was invited to perform France's national anthem for the Bastille Day parade, and while many American singers have sung in French, Jessye Norman's rendition of the Marseillaise is perhaps the most famous example. Famous French-American couples include Marilyn Monroe and Yves Montand, and Juliette Greco and Miles Davis.

Franco-American authors include Jack Kerouac, Robert Cormier, Grace Metalious, and Thoreau, and Will Durant, and writers from around the world have chosen to write in French, including Americans. Anglophone authors Samuel Beckett, Julian Green, and Jonathan Littell wrote in French. French books in translation are popular around the world, and also in the US.

Social and Cultural Networks

In alignment with the ongoing relationship between the French and the Americans, there are many social and cultural associations focusing on different aspects of this multifaceted relationship. The French Heritage Society, with ten chapters across the US, has preservation as a focus, also offering opportunities for exchanges and visits bringing the French and Americans together.

The French-American Chamber of Commerce (FACC), with 20 chapters and 4,000 members in the US and a focus on the fact that France is the third most important European trading partner of the US, promotes economic ties between the US and France and supports its member organizations as they develop their business in both the US and France. The FACC is part of the CCI France International network, with 124 chambers in 93 countries (CCI France International).

With the goal of promoting the French language and Francophone culture, the *Alliance Française* is a worldwide network of more than 800 chapters in 130 countries. In the US there are 100 Alliances, serving more than 24,000 students. The French-American Cultural Exchange (FACE) Foundation, with its mission of promoting French–American relations through education and the arts, is a US nonprofit organization that operates in partnership with the Cultural Services of the French Embassy. In terms of education and language, its portfolio includes the French dual-language fund, the French dual-language program, and the French heritage language program. The French-American Cultural Foundation promotes both cultural and commercial French and American partnerships.

In addition to 10 French Consuls in the US, there are also 56 Honorary Consuls of France in the US, recommended by the local consulate and approved by the French government, volunteers who are either of French or American nationality, who support the consulates in assisting French students, visitors, and travelers, etc.

The French are among the most frequent recipients of the Nobel Prize, ranking fourth in the world, with 69 winners with 17 in literature alone, followed closely by physics and physiology/medicine, 10 Nobel Peace prize winners, then Chemistry and Economics. Its University of Paris and *École normale supérieure* are among the universities where the most Nobel Prizes are awarded.

French Food in the US

While we may think of high-profile French eateries in major cities as the representatives of French food/cuisine in the US, it is interesting to note that Julia Child brought the idea of French cooking for the home cook to the US with her *Mastering the Art of French Cooking*, and that *Let's Eat France* was the focus of a book tour in the US in 2018 (Gaudry, 2018). While Michelin-starred restaurants and others continue to flourish in the US, the idea and practice of French cuisine pervades eateries of all types in communities large and small.

Thomas Jefferson may have brought the principles of French cuisine to the US, but the current story of French food and its influence in the US can be traced to the voyages by American food writers and experts to France, where they absorbed, embraced, and then brought back to the US an entirely different approach to food, and to eating, which formed the foundation of not only a decades-long love affair with French food but also a revolution in American food. These visionaries and influencers include MFK Fisher, Julia Child, and others.

Not only did they bring French food and the approach to food to the US, but they also transformed the American food scene for decades to come (Barr, 2014; Spring, 2017), as evidenced also by the book and film, *Julie and Julia*.

While traditional French dishes such as boeuf bourguignon, soupe à l'oignon, coq au vin, cassoulet, ratatouille, tarte tatin, and chocolate soufflé appealed to Americans, newer favorites like quiche and even more recently, macarons, appealed to a newer generation of French food fans. Beyond the era of these culinary icons, French cuisine continues to capture the imagination of Americans, whether through bistronomie, the cronut, or countless creative variations yet to come.

While many of us may be aware of the origin of the American "French fries" and the fact that the very words "restaurant" and "café" come to us directly from French, many of us are unaware that the very concept of eating as a pleasure – fine dining, or gastronomy – comes to us from the French (Brillat-Savarin), and the very idea of eating outside the home – and having trained professionals prepare our meals – comes to us directly from Paris.

The concept of *terroir*, an early part of discussions of French wines, has now expanded in definition to include the importance of soil, sunlight, weather, and other environmental factors on fruits and vegetables, meats, and dairy products – all sorts of foods. It is interesting to note that, as a result of the phylloxera epidemic that impacted French vineyards and wine production in the mid-19th century, French wine is, to some extent at least, American. An introduction to French wine in the US might include champagne, a white wine from the Loire Valley, red and white burgundy, and a *Côtes du Rhône*. An example of the popularity of French wine in the US would be the Beaujolais nouveau promotion each Fall), and while French wine is special and unique because of the *terroir* and its micro climate, global warming has already impacted it. French cheeses popular in the US include *Brie, Camembert, Comté, Chèvre, and Roquefort*, although only the pasteurized versions are generally available in the US.

While French food was widely admired, served, and imitated across the US, it is actually the French approach to food and eating, characterized by the appreciation and use of regional and in-season foods, as well as the *terroir*, or regional cuisine, that actually influenced American food and cooking at a deeper level and in a more lasting manner. It is only fitting that four of the top five restaurants in Zagat's NYC 2020 are French – Le Bernardin, Daniel, Bouley at Home, and Gabriel Kreuther (Zagat, 2019). However, lists of the best French restaurants in the US include restaurants in all parts of the country. In addition, the US is the #1 importer of French wine and spirits, and French champagne *Moët et Chandon* has been a sponsor of the New York City New Year's Eve celebration.

French Influence on Fashion in the US

More time cooking, more time at the table, and "slow cooking" are all terms that could be used to describe differences between the French and US approaches to food, but French influence also makes itself felt in the world of fashion. While the recent acquisition of the iconic US retailer, Tiffany, by the French LVMH, made news headlines, the French have long been renowned for fashion and for their sense of style. The very idea of the "fashionista" or fashion trendsetter comes to us from Paris during the era of Louis XIV, as do the essential elements of hair styling, perfume, as well as restaurants, cafés, parties, entertaining, and nightlife where we can see and be seen (De Jean, 2005).

While French fashion has long influenced the US, attracting countless American women to purchase fashions in Paris to bring them back home in the 19th century, the approach of the typical French person toward fashion is quite different that the approach of an American – the French person using fashion to create their own personal and seemingly effortless style, while the American will typically have more, but possibly lesser quality, items of clothing and accessories. Our own stylish coffee sellers find inspiration in the chic cafés of Paris. The choice of the diamond as the traditional gemstone of choice for an American engagement ring builds on the prominence of the diamond as the jewel of choice in the court of Louis XIV at Versailles. Even the mirrors, through which to better admire ourselves, are French in origin, as the French adopted the Venetian craft and made it more generally accessible. Even the modern concept of shopping comes to use from the Paris of Louis XIV. No matter how fashionable we may be, the very essence of style is French (De Jean, 2005).

Countless Americans were among the earliest visitors to the Louvre, and Paris attracted American artists, writers, and thinkers throughout the 19th century and into the 20th century (McCullough, 2011). Even in the 21st century, French artists like Monet influence our everyday lives, the color choices in home décor, and our garden and dining choices (Bordman, 2018). While it must be remembered that movies are a French invention, with an original movie camera invented by the *Frères Lumière*, many French movies have enjoyed considerable popularity in the US, and several have been remade in the US. Among the top-grossing French films in the US are *The Artist*, *Amélie*, and *La Cage aux Folles*.

Beyond the US – French and Francophone Culture in North America

While the French language and Francophone culture are an integral part of US history and cultural identity, past and present, the French language is widely used and vibrant Francophone cultures exist nearby, just beyond our borders, in Canada, and in Saint-Pierre and Miquelon, just off the coast of Canada, and in Caribbean islands including Martinique, Guadeloupe, and Saint-Martin. Beyond the US, French is used throughout the Americas, an official language and spoken by 8M in Canada, primarily in Québec; in the North Atlantic islands of Saint-Pierre and Miquelon, just off the coast of Canada; in the Caribbean, primarily in Saint-Martin, Guadeloupe, Martinique, and Haiti; in South America, primarily in Guyane.

The *Centre de la Francophonie des Amériques* (CFA) results from the leadership role of Québec in French-speaking North America. There are 33M Francophones in the Americas and 20 francophone universities in Canada. French is a required subject for high school students in Costa Rica. There are over 1,000 universities in well over 100 countries that are members of the *Agence universitaire de la Francophonie* (AUF), including many in the Americas.

Over 7M Canadians, over 20% of the population of Canada, speak French as their native language. In Québec, over three quarters of the population speak French as their mother tongue and virtually all the others speak French as a second language. About 1M Francophone Canadians live in other parts of the country, primarily in New Brunswick where about a third of the population is Francophone. Ontario, which also borders Québec, and Manitoba have a smaller percentage (fewer than 10%) of the population that is Francophone. The remaining Francophone Canadians can be found across the country. With a population of 8.5M, Québec is Canada's second largest province.

The presence of French in Canada dates back to the earliest period of French exploration on North America, with the city of Québec founded in 1608 by French explorer, Samuel de Champlain. However, the loss of Battle of Québec in 1759 was a turning point in the French–British conflict in North America, and influenced the history of Québec and of the French language in North America. The Treaty of Paris in 1763 brought Canada under British rule.

For over 200 years, with little contact with France, the French Canadians successfully maintained their language and culture despite the migration of approximately 1M French Canadians to the US, largely to New England from the mid-19th until the mid-20th century. The

Quiet Revolution, a period of great socioeconomic change in Québec during the 1960s, brought with it the rise of an independentist, or separatist movement, and continued with the election of the Parti Québécois, a separatist party under the leadership of René Lévesque, in 1970, followed more recently by Law 101, making French the sole official language of Québec, and the rise of the Bloc Québécois to political prominence.

However, in 1967, French President de Gaulle, the leader of the Free French during World War II, made the famous statement, "Vive le Québec libre!" during his 1967 speech in Montreal. It was not until 1969, with the Official Languages Act, that French achieved equal status with English as an official language of Canada, and since the early 1970s French immersion programs have increased in popularity across Canada.

Although Canada is our closest neighbor, sharing with the US the longest land border in the world, many Americans are relatively unaware that it is officially bilingual, with French and English as its official languages, and that a vibrant Francophone culture is so close. Even more Americans are unaware of the historical ties between the US and French Canada. Historically, much of what is now the US was once part of Nouvelle-France, reflected in place names including Detroit, St. Louis, and New Orleans. Even part of what is now Maine was at one time considered part of Canada and the subject of a border dispute resolved by the Webster–Ashburton Treaty of 1842.

Even more importantly in terms of the French language and Francophone culture in the US, during the period between 1840 and 1930, nearly 1M French Canadians came to the US, primarily to New England. For several generations, Francophone communities resisted assimilation through their churches, local French-language press, and through a belief in *survivance*. Today many young Americans reconnect with their cultural heritage, no longer through the past, but rather through contemporary Québec and Francophone Canada. Famous Franco-Americans include author Jack Kerouac

In addition to Québec, Francophone culture can be found throughout Canada, especially in New Brunswick and Ontario, and the deportations of the Acadians to Louisiana in the period following the Fall of Québec and the end of the French colonial Empire in Canada led to the existence of Cajun (a form of the word Acadian) culture in Louisiana. The subsequent purchase of Louisiana, which included much of the Mississippi Valley, that had been part of *la Nouvelle France*, brought Acadian culture into the US cultural experience.

The US Francophonie is a complex culture heritage, including descendants of the earliest French explorers and settlers, refugees fleeing the French Revolution and its aftermath from both France and the Caribbean, followed French-Canadian immigrants to New England (both Québécois and Acadien) over the period of a century ending in the early- to mid-20th century, as well as more recent arrivals from France, the Caribbean, and Francophone Africa. An interesting initiative, and exciting step forward, was the entry of the state of Louisiana into the Francophonie in 2018 (Louisiana Joins, 2018).

In close proximity to the US, the islands of Saint-Pierre and Miquelon, formally part of metropolitan France, lie just off the Atlantic coast of Canada. In the Caribbean, Francophone islands including Martinique, Guadeloupe, Saint-Martin and other islands that are part of Metropolitan France, as well as Haiti, are easily accessible from the US. In addition, significant numbers of Haitians have made their home in the US, and French/Haitian Creole is widely spoken in South Florida, the New York area, and in other parts of the US. Nearly 1M Haitian Americans live in the US. Saint-Pierre and Miquelon, with a population today of just over 6,000, were ceded to Britain with the Treaty of Paris, but were returned to France.

Conclusions

The Francophone presence in the US includes heritage communities and new Americans, as well as French speakers from France and throughout the Francophone world. While the interconnectedness of the globalized world has transformed the Francophone space in the US, it is important to remember the presence or 33M Francophones throughout the Americas and the presence of French-speaking populations adjacent to the US – in Canada, Saint-Pierre and Miquelon, the Caribbean, and in Latin America.

Our French heritage and historical relationship with French language and culture are strengthened and transformed by the Francophone presence within and adjacent to the US and by the increasing access to travel and to authentic information and entertainment.

4 The Global Francophone Environment
Trends and Analysis

Introduction

French is a global language, and has been for centuries. French language and culture have long been respected and admired, and French lifestyle continues to draw international visitors to France from around the world. The *Organisation internationale de la Francophonie* (OIF), with nearly 90 members worldwide, is grounded in not only the French language but also in the humanistic values of France and the Francophone world. French "soft power" or influence is strong (Gray, 2017), and French books, movies, and television series are among the most popular in the world. France is one of the world's largest economies, Francophone regions account for about a fifth of world trade (OIF, 2014, 2018), and French is considered one of the top languages of business (English, Chinese, and French, 2011). The number of French speakers is increasing throughout the world, with French predicted to possibly become the most widely spoken language in the world by mid-21st century, and French is the second most learned foreign language in the world. In a multilingual world, French – existing largely in a multilingual environment – is the quintessential 21st-century language. The French language, an official language of the United Nations, the International Olympic Committee, and many other international organizations, plays a significant role in international discussions and relations, Brexit has raised the question of a strengthened role of French within the European Union (Brexit: English Language Losing Importance, 2017; Heath, 2017; Kanter & Vogelenter, 2017), and the French government launched a campaign for the worldwide promotion of French in 2018. In 2021, the online *Dictionnaire des Francophones*, highlighting the role of French speakers around the world as Francophone stakeholders, was launched (New French Dictionary, 2021).

DOI: 10.4324/9781003023760-5

French is spoken around the world, present on the five continents, and used on a daily basis by nearly 250M people around the world. The OIF has 88 member states and governments (OIF, 2014, 2018). French has been predicted to be the most widely spoken language in Europe in a few years and to be the most widely spoken language in the world by mid-century (Gobry, 2014). French was an official language of the League of Nations and has been an official language of the United Nations, of which it is one of two working languages of the UN Secretariat. It is also an official language of the European Union. It is one of two official languages of the International Olympic Committee and is an official language of many international organizations. French is an official or widely used language in many countries beyond French borders, including Belgium, Switzerland, Monaco, and Luxembourg in Europe, and many areas beyond Europe throughout the world, with the largest number and growth rate in Africa. The French government, with its dual-language immersion initiative and many other activities, has been an active supporter of French language learning around the world and in 2018 launched a campaign for the promotion of French in the world.

The French Language in the World

In addition to being an official or prevalent language around the world, French is a language of information, entertainment, education, the workplace, and daily life around the world. French is the language of communication used in media around the world, French films and television series attract audiences worldwide, students worldwide seek education in French schools and institutions of higher learning, French is among the most useful languages for international business, and people around the world use French in their daily lives, homes, and communities. French is the second most widely learned language in the world, and the number of French speakers in the world is growing exponentially.

French is present on five continents, but to varying degrees, ranging from an official or prevalent language, or a language used widely in education, business, and social life, to language spoken only by specific groups, or learned as a foreign language in school. French speakers include those who use French on a daily or regular basis, as well as those who use French more occasionally. Over half of the daily speakers of French live in Africa, followed by Europe, with about a third of daily speakers. North Africa/Middle East and Europe are leaders in terms of the number of students learning French as a foreign language, and

Africa and Asia/Oceania are the areas with the fastest growth rate. Over 30 countries use French as a language of instruction, usually in conjunction with a local language. French is among the top three languages in international business. International media in French includes TV5Monde, Radio France Internationale (RFI), France 24, Euronews, and many more, and French is among the top languages on the internet, Wikipedia, and even Amazon. French is an official of many international organizations, including the UN, EU, International Olympic Committee, and many more. French is the third most powerful language in the world (Chan, 2016).

The status of French varies from country to country, ranging from status as an official language or a widely used language, to a language spoken by specific groups. The language itself changes as well, with one standard French language used internationally, with, however, local accents, words, expressions, and ways of speaking. These local variations are the norm within languages spoken over wide areas of the world, as is the case with French, and in no way detract from the global role and significance of French as a world language.

In terms of the French language beyond the *Hexagone*, it is first important to remember that there are areas scattered throughout the world that are actually part of Metropolitan France, with French as official language. Beyond France, French is an official language in areas geographically bordering France, reflecting the relatively frequent lack of alignment between current political boundaries and language communities.

The Worldwide Campaign for French

Building on French "soft power" or influence and on the status of French as a global language, following a worldwide consultation, French President Emmanuel Macron announced a worldwide campaign for the promotion of French on the occasion of the *Journée internationale de la Francophonie* 2018. This campaign would be framed by French language learning, French as a language of communication, and French as a language of creativity. In 2020, the restoration of Château de Villers-Cotterêts as a center for this language campaign began, and is significant in the symbolism of the use of the site of the 1539 *Ordonnance de Villers-Cotterêts* which marked the beginning of the expansion of French into its current role as the official national language of France (France Diplomacy, Institutions Promoting, 2019; Franceinfo, 2021; Macron Turns Derelict Chateau, 2018).

While the current status of French as a global language of culture, communication, education, and information, as well as its status as the second most studied language in the world would seem to indicate that a campaign for its promotion would be unnecessary, the relative status and influence of languages are constantly changing due to a variety of factors including political and economic power, as well as "soft power" or influence (Peckham, n.d.).

Global and Regional Francophone Organizations

While the OIF is perhaps the best known of the many organizations representing and involving French language and Francophone culture around the world, there are numerous regional and local organizations with complementary goals, including the *Centre de la francophonie des Amériques*.

The OIF, founded as the *Agence de Coopération Culturelle et Technique* in 1970, and intended to foster and encourage cooperation among nations and regions where French was a prevalent language based on a shared language and values, celebrated its 50th anniversary in 2020. It is important to note, however, that the promotion of French language and humanistic values is grounded in the concept of global multilingualism and support of local languages. Léopold Senghor, President of Sénégal, was an early supporter, its leadership position of Secretary-General has been occupied by many high-profile figures, and recent Secretaries-General have included Abdou Diouf (Sénégal), Michaëlle Jean (Canada), and Louise Mushikiwabo (Rwanda). Active in many areas, it is best known internationally for its *Jeux de la Francophonie*, held every four years and hosted in a member state or region; the *Journée internationale de la Francophonie*, observed on March 20th and the centerpiece of the *Mois de la Francophonie*; and TV5Monde available throughout the world. In the US, it is perhaps best known for the fact that in 2018, the state of Louisiana became a member. Most recently, the OIF has published a report, *La Francophonie de l'avenir*, based on a consultative survey of more than 10,000 young people in over 80 member states and regions (OIF).

The *Centre de la Francophonie des Amériques*, located in Québec, has as its mission to bring together and to build a bridge among diverse Francophone communities throughout the Americas, which it does through a variety of programs and initiatives, including the *Réseau des villes francophones et francophiles*, which has undergone transition following the global pandemic (Boutroy, 2021).

The Global Francophone Environment 41

It is interesting to examine the reasons why French is spoken so widely beyond French borders and why it is so appealing to language learners everywhere. The terms "Francophile" and "Francophone," referring to those who love France, French, and all things relating to French and Francophone culture in the world and to those who speak and use French, respectively, have worldwide significance through the centuries. French President Macron has spoken convincingly of the *attractivité* or appeal, of French, but the story of French as a language used by more people around the world than actually live in France is a very modern story that has its roots in history. In addition to global and regional organizations bringing together Francophone communities, there are also local associations and initiatives. In the US, these include the Franco-American Centre of New Hampshire (FACNH) and the Council for the Development of French in Louisiana (CODO-FIL) at the state level, the Nous Foundation in the city of New Orleans, and the France Heritage Foundation of Minnesota and many others.

French Language and Culture in the World

While French culture has been admired, and the French language has been widely learned for centuries, globalization has highlighted the international role of languages. In addition, French is characterized by often existing alongside one or more languages rather than as the sole language in a country or region. Because of this long-standing and widespread interest and affection for French language and culture that crosses many borders, terms like Francophile and Francophilia have been used to describe them. An example of this would be the prevalence of French as a language of communication among the elite in Russia in the 18th and 19th century, some of which can be seen in 19th-century novels, including *War and Peace.*

However, there are two unique institutions, the *Institut Français* and the *Alliance Française*, that exist to promote French language and culture throughout the world. *The Institut Français* was established by the French government in 1907 in order to promote French and Francophone cultures around the world. Since 2011, it has had an even broader mission to promote French culture around the world through artistic and cultural exchanges. The *Alliance Française*, created in 1883, is an international organization that works to promote French language and culture around the world (Alliance Française, n.d.; Institut Français, n.d.).

With well over 800 branches around the world in 132 countries and on 5 continents, the *Alliance Française* has as its mission to offer

French courses, to promote French and Francophone culture, and to foster cultural diversity. It is interesting to note that, with over 150 Alliances, the US is the world leader in terms of the number of Alliances. On the other hand, the AF in Havana, Cuba, leads in terms of the number of French learners. Among the top ten countries in terms of the number of Alliances, four are in the Americas (US, Argentina, Brazil, and Mexico), and four are in Europe (Italy, the Netherlands, France, and Spain), with Madagascar and Australia 7th and 8th on the list (Les Alliances Françaises dans le Monde, 2017).

French as a Global Language of Education

Insofar as French as a language of education is concerned, in addition to those around the world who learn French as an additional, second, or foreign language, it is essential to consider those who are educated in French, in French language schools around the world.

The Agency for French Education Abroad (AEFE, 2021) is an entity of the French government charged with the dual mission of ensuring that the children of French nationals abroad receive a French education and of supporting French language and cultural learning around the world. This system includes well over 500 schools abroad with an enrollment of nearly 400,000 students from nursery school through high school in nearly 150 countries, and well over half the students enrolled are foreign nationals. In addition to language and cultural learning, the institutions – through their worldwide alumni – international understanding and cooperation (AEFE, 2019). It is also important to remember the many private schools around the world where French language and cultural knowledge are emphasized, including the Lycée Français de New York (Ross, 2020).

Within the context of the French government initiative to promote French throughout the world, Africa – home to a majority of the French speakers in the world – has received particular attention. Beyond the network of French schools abroad, there are two programs specifically intended to foster and encourage French as a medium of instruction in a multilingual learning environment in schools in Africa – ELAN and IFADEM. ELAN (*École et langues nationales en Afrique*) is intended to support the use of French and local languages in a multilingual learning environment. IFADEM (*L'Initiative francophone pour la formation à distance des maîtres*), an initiative of the *Agence universitaire de la Francophonie* (AUF) and the OIF, is intended to develop training programs for teachers in various African countries to teach in French within a context that is in alignment with local educational structures and objectives (France Diplomacy, French External Action, 2010; Marshall, 2011).

French culture is known and appreciated around the world, and the French language is spoken on a daily basis by 235M, making it the fifth most widely spoken language in the world. The OIF, founded in 1970, has 88 members, 22 observers, on 5 continents, in 160 countries and territories. Fifty-nine percent of its daily speakers live in Africa. 51M are learning French as a foreign language, of which 45% are in North Africa and the Middle East. Another 81M are learning in French, with French as the language of instruction, of which 72.8% are in Africa. French is used in education, in the workplace, in business, and in the hotel and tourism sector. The influence of French in the world includes 1.2B inhabitants, 16% of the world population, and 16.5% of the world's wealth. French is the fourth most frequently used language on the internet. Today, 300M speak French, predicted to rise to 747M by 2070 (OIF, 2014, 2018). French is a language of international communication, an official language of many international organizations including the International Olympic Committee, the United Nations, and the European Union. It is also a language of the internet and online and broadcast media, including TV5Monde, RFI, France 24, with tens of millions of viewers and listeners around the world. In bilingual Canada, Francophone Radio-Canada exists alongside its Anglophone counterpart, the CBC. In 2018, French President Emmanuel Macron launched an initiative to promote the French language worldwide. March 20th is the International Francophone Day, with programs and events throughout the French-speaking world.

French as a Global Language and as a Global Competency

France is one of the top two countries in the world with the most cultural influence, ranking second in the world only following Italy, which means that it is a "cultural trendsetter" (France Ranked World's Top Cultural Trendsetter, 2016), whose ideas, fashion, entertainment, and lifestyle are widely emulated and play a significant role in the wider global conversation. French inventions and innovations that have become part of daily life include the stethoscope, photography, movie camera, pasteurization, the sewing machine, Braille, and aspirin (McFadden, 2020).

France is the most visited country by foreign tourists in the world, and there is even a specific term, "francophilia," to describe those who admire France, its language, and its culture. Francophiles are to be found around the world, and the presence of the *Alliance Française* in 132 countries is just one indicator of the extent of admiration for French culture. In fact, Francophiles have long existed, drawn to the lights and court life of France during the era of Louis XIV, to the ideas of the enlightenment, its literature and art throughout the centuries, as well as to its cuisine.

French influence is felt throughout the world, especially in areas that have historic ties to France and former colonies, and especially through various aid programs in Africa and the Middle East. The government of Jamaica in 2019 launched a French language initiative intended to promote ties between the English- and French-speaking Caribbean. France is an active participant in many international organizations, exerting influence through cooperation. While the concepts of Francophile and Francophone are not the same, they may often coincide, and the OIF is an interesting example of an organization whose members are tied together by not only a common language, French, but also by the French tradition of humanistic values.

In addition to being the language of France, French is spoken around the world by 300M, of whom 235M speak it on a daily basis, including 2M in the US who speak French or French Creole at home. It is an official language of many international organizations, including the United Nations, the European Union, and the International Olympic Committee. It is the focus of the OIF, which has 88 members and observers around the world. French is one of the most powerful languages in the world, and one of the most useful languages for international business.

It is one of the most widely spoken languages in the world, spoken in over 100 countries and territories. Over half of the daily speakers of French live in Africa. French is also learned as a foreign language, through the network of *Instituts français* and *Alliances françaises*, as well as through school systems and universities, with 51M learners around the world, and 81M students studying in institutions using French as the language of instruction. For many, French is the language of education, business, and the workplace – the language of their future, providing access to careers in tourism, and to international careers (Palet, 2014).

In addition, French online, print, and social media provide access to news, information, and entertainment to millions, and French literature, art, and music are world-renowned. In fact, French literary prizes have been awarded to authors from outside France, writing in French, reflecting the global nature of the language and its use. French soft power and influence are especially important in terms of the relationships France has developed and maintains around the world.

The French Language in Africa, Europe, Asia, and the Americas

French is widely spoken throughout Africa, either as an official or widely spoken or prevalent language. Africa is home to the largest number of French speakers in the world, with well over half of those who use French on a daily basis. It is interesting to note the significant role of Africa in the creation and history of the OIF, with President of Sénégal Léopold Senghor an early proponent and supporter of the OIF. France is a leader in foreign direct investment (FDI) and in trade with Africa, an active supporter of multilingual education, and French business organizations provide professional training for their many workers. It is interesting to note that French President Macron had a student internship in Africa, made the announcement of the worldwide campaign for the French language while in Africa, and that French-Senegalese Sibeth Ndiaye has served as government spokesperson within his government.

French is widely spoken throughout Europe, both by mother tongue speakers and by French language learners, with more than 45% of daily speakers located in Europe. It is necessary to remember that in addition to being the historical home of French, that generally most students study one or more additional languages from an early age. Above all, it is important to note that – beyond France – French typically exists in a multilingual environment, coexisting with one or more local or national languages. Europe is the home of French. The French language is descended from Latin, and a member of the Romance language family that includes Spanish, Italian, Portuguese, Romanian, Catalan, and Romansh, etc. The language that the world knows as French began its journey toward becoming the national language with the *Ordonnance de Villers-Cotterêts* in 1539, supported by the *Académie Française*, and known for its literature and as a language of ideas and culture.

The French language is an important language in the European space and the European Union. While French has long been an important language in Europe, France, Switzerland, Belgium, Monaco, and Luxembourg, and widely spoken throughout Europe, the recent exit of the United Kingdom from the European Union has resulted in a marked increase in the role of French. Just a few years ago, European Commission President Juncker noted the decline of English as a European language, and this has been again precipitated by the conclusion of Brexit (Heath, 2017; Kanter & Wolgelenter, 2017).

French is an official language in Switzerland, Belgium, Luxembourg, and Monaco. French is predominant in the western part of

Switzerland including Geneva often referred to as *la Suisse romande*, which borders France, but widely taught throughout the country along with German and Italian, the other official languages. A fourth national language, Romansh, is spoken by a relatively small number of Swiss. Multilingualism has a long history in Switzerland and is generally a source of pride and viewed as an asset (Federal Council, n.d.; Wolfestone, n.d.). However, as French is the mother tongue of slightly more than 20% of the population, it is not the predominant language nationally, with German the mother tongue of more than 60% of the population. A challenge is to maintain a balance between the tradition of providing government services in the mother tongue of each Swiss and the reality of the preponderance of German as a mother tongue of the majority of Swiss a major presence is government and business.

French is the official language of the French Community in Belgium and the predominant language in the southern region of Wallonia, which borders France. Although Brussels the national capital is geographically located outside the predominantly Francophone region, its role as capital and its role in the EU result in French being a major presence there.

It is noteworthy that it is only in recent years that Belgium had its first Francophone Prime Minister, Elio Di Rupo, from 2011 to 2014.

French is also an official language of two smaller nations, Monaco and Luxembourg, n.d.). French is the official language in Monaco, a principality that is located on the Mediterranean coast near the Italian border and is well known as a resort with beautiful beaches and casinos. Additional languages spoken include Monegasque and English. French is an official language in Luxembourg, widely used in this nation characterized by the international character of its business sector. An official language in areas that have maintained an official relationship with France, including New Caledonia, Vanuatu, and French Polynesia, French is also widely spoken, especially in Southeast Asia.

The French language and Francophone culture are vibrant forces throughout the Americas. An official language in Canada, in Saint-Pierre and Miquelon, in the Caribbean, and in South America, it is spoken by over 33M throughout the Americas. French is spoken by more than 2M in the home in the US, where over 10M claim French ancestry. An additional factor to consider in the US is the surge in the number of expats and immigrants from French-speaking areas to regions across the US. In addition, it is necessary to take into consideration the significant number of Francophiles and French language learners throughout the Americas. With a mission of bringing together the diverse Francophone community in the Americas, the *Centre de la francophonie des Amériques* (CFA) is headquartered in Québec.

For French language supporters and advocates in North America and beyond, the story of Québec, of Canada, and of official bilingualism is both an example of French language advocacy and a wonderful success story. Because of its North American context and proximity to the US, the story of French in Canada can offer inspiration to Francophones and Franco-Americans, many of whom are of Québécois or Acadian ancestry, despite the real differences between both nations in terms of both history and society.

Much of what is today Canada and the US was part of *la Nouvelle France* from the earliest days of European exploration of North America until the Fall of Québec to the British in 1759. However, French has been an official language of all of Canada since 1969, and the official language of Québec since the passage of the *Charter of the French Language (La charte de la langue française)*, also known as *La Loi 101* in 1977, which ensures language rights to Francophones.

After the fall of Québec in 1759, Québec and the inhabitants of the former *Nouvelle France* were separated from France and part of a larger British colony for over a century, then part of a largely Anglophone Canada, which only in 1969 promulgated the Official Languages Act, finally making all of Canada officially bilingual.

In Québec, however, after *la Révolution tranquille* and French President De Gaulle's proclamation *Vive le Québec libre!* during a visit to Québec, the *Parti Québécois* was able to enact *La Loi 101* to protect the French language in Québec. However, while it would not be difficult to imagine that the future of French in Québec and in Canada would be assured with both the Federal and Provincial legislations in place, the fact remains that more than 50 years after the Official Languages Act, it has been said that French was largely sidelined during the COVID crisis in spring 2020 in Québec, Ontario, and New Brunswick, and the Québec government has recently needed to introduce additional measures to safeguard French. Existing in a multilingual environment, as French does throughout the world beyond French borders, French is often at risk, or in question, and French language supporters around the world must continue to be constantly vigilant.

In terms of the percentage of Francophones, Québec and New Brunswick have the greatest percentage of Francophones. In Québec, 6,890,305 (85.4%), and in New Brunswick, 234,055 (31.8%) are Francophone, with fewer than 5% of the Francophone population in the remaining provinces. However, Ontario, where 550,595 (4.1%) are

Francophone, the number of Francophones is significant. Nationally, 7,914,498 (22.8%) of the population is Francophone (Statistics, 2019).

While French is an official language throughout Canada, beyond Québec, education and other services in French may vary in terms of their availability. French immersion programs, in existence since the 1960s, continue to be popular and sought-after, with some 309,000 students (7.7% of total eligible enrollment) were enrolled between JK and Grade 12, more than a third of them in Ontario. Certain places, including parts of British Columbia and areas of Toronto, are experiencing sharp rates of growth, reflecting the fact that it is well known that bilinguals earn more (Daniellson, 2017).

Conclusions

Building on the historical significance of the French language and culture, along with the *attractivité*, or appeal, of French culture, ideas, and lifestyle in the world today, French "soft power" or influence plays a role in the importance of the French language and Francophone culture in the world today (Gray, 2017). Already considered one of the most powerful languages in the world (Chan, 2016), the number of French speakers in the world is increasing, and French has been predicted to be the most widely spoken language in the world by mid-21st century (Gobry, 2014).

The future of French is bright, based on the appeal of the lifestyle, culture, ideas, and values that it represents within France and throughout the world (Palet, 2014). Ensuring that French language learning is available to children throughout the world is key to future success, most strikingly characterized by multilingual and dual-language immersion programs in many countries, including the US, is an essential first step. Further leveraging the appeal of French language and Francophone cultures through communication and creativity – through information, education, media, business use, etc., as well as through entertainment and the arts – are next steps in developing a sustainable future for French language and Francophone culture in the world.

5 The Economic Impact of French as a Global and Local Business Language

Introduction

The economic impact of French as a global and local business language is undeniable. Not only is France one of the world's largest economies and Francophone regions of the world do account for nearly 20% of global trade (OIF, 2014, 2018), French is considered one of the most powerful languages in the world, one of the most important languages for international business, and one of the most sought-after languages in the US workplace (ACTFL, 2019; Chan, 2016; English, Chinese, and French, 2011; NAE, 2017). France is a major trading partner of the US, and approximately 5,000 French companies operate in the US. French companies employ approximately 750K workers in the US, and US companies employ a similar number in France (French Treasury, 2017, 2019; Thiery, 2018).

France is a global leader in the automotive, aerospace, and railway sectors as well as in beauty and luxury goods, with French brands including Renault, Airbus, and most recently, Bombardier, and in the beauty and luxury sector, Louis Vuitton, l'Oréal, Dior, and more. The educational sector supports the French economy as well, and France is known for its highly educated labor force, with a high number of college educated in the sciences. It would be nearly impossible to spend any length of time without coming into contact with a French product, company, or concept in the marketplace or workplace, whether that product has a name or label well known to be French, or whether it is a product or service developed and marketed by a local partner or subsidiary of a French multinational.

As a member of the EU, France's most important trading partner is Germany. In terms of international trade, France's main exports are machinery and transportation equipment, aerospace equipment, and plastics (European Union, France, n.d.). As France is the most visited

DOI: 10.4324/9781003023760-6

country in the world, another demonstration of the soft power and appeal of French lifestyle and culture, tourism is a major economic sector. In juxtaposition and in as a complement to its global role, France has worked to uphold and support its culture and language, implementing the *loi Toubon*, which requires the use of French in a wide range of business, educational, legal, and media environments. France is an attractive destination for, and a leader in, foreign direct investment (FDI), and many believe that Brexit offers an opportunity for France. With innovation a driver, the economic appeal and attractiveness of France is based in its infrastructure, educated workforce, market size, economic stability, and overall business environment. In addition, its open business environment, quality of life, and tradition of entrepreneurship are additional factors in its global appeal (France Diplomacy, Entrepreneurship and Investing, 2019).

Just as language is the foundation of effective communication in any organization, including businesses and companies, languages play a central role in communication in the multilingual business environment whether locally or internationally, both on the customer or client side in terms of service and marketing, and on the operations side where a diversity of perspective and thought plays a critical role in success (Livermore, 2016). In addition, a shared language can bring together potential partners across regional and national boundaries, well illustrated by the multiple relationships among countries in the Anglosphere, the Francophonie, or any other language-related group. Language plays a significant role in competitiveness, with the six official languages of the UN among the most powerful languages in the world (Chan, 2016). French is among the top three languages useful in international business, and among the top languages in demand among US employers (ACTFL, 2019; English, Chinese, and French, 2011; NAE, 2017). Multilingualism and language education are at the foundation of economic success, and French is the second most learned language in the world. Economic *francophonie* is an advantage in many ways, facilitating communication, teamwork, as well as expansion and success in new markets (Carrere, 2014).

France is a major economic power, and French is considered one of the useful languages for international business, as well as one of the most influential languages in the world (English, Chinese, French, 2011; Chan, 2016). Francophone nations and regions around the world include a population of 1B potential partners, customers, and consumers for businesses everywhere. French is the fifth most widely spoken language in the world, with a presence on the five continents, and is considered an asset in terms of access to education and information, as well as a personal and career asset. As a language of business, more than 20% of international trade takes place among areas where French is prevalent. French media reach present and potential markets worldwide, and French is among the most important languages on the internet, on Wikipedia, and on Amazon (OIF, 2014, 2018). 25 French companies are part of the Fortune Global 500, with Total, AXA, Carrefour, Credit Agricole, and Peugeot leading the list (Fortune Global, 2020). The most valuable French brands include Louis Vuitton, Chanel, Hermes, L'Oreal Paris, and Orange. Bernard Arnault, the CEO of LVMH Moët Hennessy – Louis Vuitton SE, the world's largest luxury goods company, has been considered the richest man in the world.

France is among the most attractive countries for FDI in the world. It is a global economic power, open to investors. It is centrally located in the EU, and Paris is a leading European financial center. France is known as a nation of entrepreneurs, has a highly educated and qualified workforce, and most importantly, is known for innovation and its start-ups. In terms of global competitiveness, France has ranked 15th in the world. In addition, French "soft power," or influence has been the ranked the first in the world (Gray, 2017; Schwab, 2019; USNews, The Best Countries, 2019). In the globalized environment, where it has become challenging for individual nations to exercise influence, France is known for its support of multilateralism. The worldwide reach of French business, and appeal of French "soft power," and the role of language in global competitiveness have made France a leader in influence and make its language a career and workplace advantage globally (Gray, 2017).

French Global Economic Influence

French companies known throughout the world include Renault, Alcatel, and Michelin, among others. Many French multinational companies earn a large part of their revenue outside France, and France is a model worldwide in its ability to adapt to globalization while continuing to support a level of social protection for the individual worker that remains a model for the world, striving to combine any benefits of globalization with the sustainability of a national economy. French areas of strength include agriculture, technology, industry, its educational system, its well-educated workforce, and the worldwide use of French as a language of international business. Major areas of the French economy include public administration, defense, education, health, retail trade, transportation, hotel and restaurant services, and professional and administrative services.

Business France and CCI International are two government initiatives intended to support, strengthen, and promote French business around the world. Business France works to foster French export growth, to support foreign investment in France, and to promote French companies and the appeal of France as an investment environment, and operates in well over 100 countries. The CCI France International, *Chambres de Commerce et d'Industrie Françaises à l'International*, has as its mission to bring together and to develop the international French Chamber of Commerce and Industry network, and operates in nearly 100 countries. Including international summits, "Choose France/*Bienvenue en France*," an initiative designed to enhance the appeal of France as a destination for businesses, FDI, start-ups, and international students, was launched in 2018 (Business France: France's Global Economy, 2018; Business France: Who are we?, n.d.; CCI France International, 2021; Choose France, 2018, 2019).

France is an active trading partner and investor throughout the world, especially within the EU and within the *Francophonie* or French-speaking world. A member of the European Union, France is one of the largest EU and Eurozone economies. Trade with EU members includes well over half of France's exports, with the US and China being major external trading partners. In terms of imports, well over half come from EU members, with the US and China being major trading partners. In Africa, Asia, and the Middle East, French economic activity exists within the context of long-standing historical relationships.

In Africa, France is an active participant in the economy as a trading partner and second most important exporter. Since 2000, French investment in Africa has increased significantly, along with it opportunities for the use of French in the workplace professional development, and related areas. Well over 1,000 French business organizations operate in Africa, with nearly a half million jobs created by French companies in North Africa alone. The French government's Business France agency has strengthened its presence in Africa in recent years to support local French businesses. The annual "Ambition Africa" event, a business forum managed by Business France, is an opportunity for African and French businesses to come together. French government also supports French–African partnerships in many areas (Business France, Ambition Africa, n.d.; France Diplomacy, Economic Relations between France and Africa, 2019).

In Asia, France has increased its level of investment and involvement in recent years (Godement, 2014). Examples of this include the France-Vietnam Business Forum in 2018, organized by French

The Economic Impact of French 53

Chamber of Commerce and Industry in Vietnam (CCIFV; Thuy, 2018); with more than 300 members, the French Job Fair was organized in 2020 by the French Chamber of Commerce in Japan (CCIFJ, 2021; CCIFV, 2021). There is also a French Companies Fair (CCIFJ, 2020). In the Middle East, trading partners include the United Arab Emirates, Saudi Arabia, Egypt, and Lebanon, and economic activity extends also to mutual FDI. With its mission of supporting and promoting the partnership between France and the Arab world, the Franco-Arab Chamber of Commerce observed its 50th anniversary in 2020. France is one of the most important business partners of Lebanon, and the most important trading partner of Tunisia (CCFA, 2021; Franco-Arab Chamber, n.d.).

In Latin America, Argentina is one of France's most important trading partners, and over 250 French companies operate in Argentina. France also partners with Argentina in many scientific research projects (France Diplomacy, France-Argentina Relations, 2016.). Many Argentinians study French, and France is a popular study abroad destination for Argentinian students. Argentina has been since 2016 an observer member of the *Organisation internationale de la Francophonie* (OIF). Mexico is an increasingly important trading partner and FDI location for France (French Companies Are Targeting Mexico to Do Business with, 2020). Brazil is a major trading partner of France, and nearly 900 subsidiaries of French companies are in Brazil (including almost all CAC 40 companies), who generate more than half a million jobs in Brazil (France Diplomacy, France and Brazil, 2021; French Companies, 2020).

In the Americas, for historical and demographic reasons, the French language plays a different role in US and in Canadian business. As French is an official language in Canada, and the official language in Québec, it is important to distinguish between French-Canadian businesses and French companies. In addition, Canada, along with Québec and New Brunswick, are members of the *Francophonie*. In Canada, Francophone businesses play a significant role in the economy, with many Francophone Canadian enterprises like Desjardins, Couche-Tard (which has attempted to acquire the French multinational Carrefour), and Bombardier (acquired by the French company, Alstom) known around the world. For nearly 75 years, the France Canada Chamber of Commerce has worked to foster economic exchanges and cooperation between France and Canada. France and Canada are important trading partners in both goods and services, and in terms of FDI. Because of its bilingual workforce, Québec is especially attractive to French companies, with Montreal an important entry point to

North America for many French enterprises, along with its digital and web industries and start-up-friendly business environment (CCFC, 2021; Dieudonne, 2017; Missions de la Chambre, n.d.).

France and the French Language in the US

French is the third most in-demand language by US employers, 22% of employers, and 29% of employers with international language needs, reporting that they need French. French is also the third most in-demand language among employers for domestic needs, and 17% of respondents cite it as being in short supply, and 13% report difficulty in finding French language skills among prospective employees. French is also among the top three languages among employers who actually test for language skills (ACTFL, 2019). In terms of use of French in the US workplace, the CODOFIL Louisiana *Oui* Initiative, and the French Jobs Fairs in New Orleans and San Diego highlight the importance of the actual use of French in the US workplace (Canone, 2019; CODOFIL, 2021; Cultural Services, 2021; Gagliano, 2019).

France and the US are major trading partners, and each is a major investor in the other. The US is the largest foreign direct investor in France, with $86.9B in FDI stock, and France is the third largest investor in the US, with $326.4B of French FDI stock in the US. France and the US traded over $129B in goods and services in the most recent year. Thousands of French companies operating in the US provide nearly 750,000 jobs in the US, and is the third largest foreign employer in the US, and American companies employ a half million people in France (French Treasury, 2017, 2019). French economic activity is strong throughout the states, with Texas and California with the highest levels of both trade and employment. Louisiana, the sole US member of the OIF, renewed the France-Louisiana Accords, a long-standing agreement with France on professional and educational initiatives in 2021 (Louisiana, France, 2021; Lt. Gov. Nungesser and CODOFIL, 2021).

The French-American Chambers of Commerce, founded in 1896, and the American Chamber of Commerce in France, founded in 1901, share 120 years of working to promote economic cooperation between the two nations (French American Chamber, n.d.; L'AmCham France, n.d.). The French American Chamber of Commerce (FACC) is a non-governmental organization, intended to promote economic cooperation between the US and France and to support French companies in the US. Located in nearly 20 cities, including New York, Atlanta, Chicago, and Los Angeles, the FACC has locations throughout the

US. The American Chamber of Commerce in France (AmCham) is an independent nonpolitical organization, and members include both CAC40 and Fortune 100 companies along with the newest start-ups.

French is the third most in-demand language other than English in the US workplace, with demand in 2015 more than double what it had been in 2010 (ACTFL, 2019; NAE, 2017). French remains especially demanded in the humanitarian sectors (NAE, 2017). In addition to being the third most highly demanded language, it is considered in short supply and difficult to find (ACTFL, 2019). French is also the third most useful language for international business (English, Chinese, and French, 2011).

France is one of the world's largest economies, a major trading partner with the US, and a major employer of US workers. France has ten consulates in the US, facilitating French commercial activity in the US and responding to the needs of the many French nationals visiting or residing in the US. Not only are there French companies operating in every state, French companies employ nearly 700,000 workers, with California, Texas, New York, and New Jersey being the states with the largest number of jobs created by French companies. US companies employ approximately the same number of workers in France. French companies employing significant numbers of American workers include Safran, Thales, Airbus, L'Oreal, Michelin, Saft, Dassault, LVMH, Air Liquide, Schneider Electric, Suez/Engie, CertainTeed (Saint-Gobain), Keolis, bioMérieux, Vallourec, Savencia, Bel, Faurecia, Total, Atos, Teleperformance, Sodexo, Cuisine Solutions, Capgemini, and more (France Treasury, 2017).

French is a language of the workplace and of careers and professions in the US, with jobs of all types across the US requiring, or enhanced by, French language skills and knowledge of French and Francophone culture. A recent search on indeed.com returned 6,973 results for French/French-speaking jobs, and a search for French bilingual jobs returned 1,040 results. "Nearly 22,300 job offers published online in 2015 in the U.S. were looking for candidates proficient in French compared to 9,500 in 2010. French is the third most requested language on the American labor market, particularly in sectors such as insurance, healthcare, finance, and humanitarian aid" (Cultural Services, What is French. n.d.).

In terms of the Francophone world beyond France, Québec is just one example of an economic and workplace partner of the US, with 255K Americans working for Québec-owned companies, more than 12,000 Québec companies doing business in the US, 66B in bilateral trade, and $3.4B spent by Québécois traveling to the US (Noreau, 2017).

Conclusions

The importance of communication and of language(s) in transnational teams and in business generally is clear (Hardach, 2018; Hogan-Brun, 2017; Livermore, 2016). As a major global economy, France and the French language play a significant role in France and the Francophone world, and beyond. It is one of the most important languages in international business, a career asset, and a language of education, career training, and information worldwide. The *Francophonie* region accounts for nearly 20% of global trade, and France and Canada are among the top trading partners of the US (Economic Relations between Canada and France, n.d.). FDI between the US and France is significant on both sides, with many French companies operating in the US and employing US workers and vice versa. The number of French speakers – and potential customers, clients, and consumers – is rapidly increasingly. However, most importantly, French ideas are most closely associated with humanistic values and multilateralism in a globalized world.

6 Bilingualism
Benefits, Opportunities, and Analysis

Introduction

In order to effectively address complex global issues, further exacerbated by the COVID-19 pandemic, we must be able to speak with each other as global citizens and as part of a global community, and a renewed commitment to the use of other languages in our society and to language learning is of critical importance in order to develop a global mindset and skills and to foster and encourage harmony at home (AMACAD, 2020).

The discussion of the French in our lives extends beyond the role of French in international organizations and multinational corporations and is grounded in the idea of bilingualism in our homes and communities, and in the life of the mind. Language plays a critical role in our worldview, and multilingualism can be the best way of developing understanding of other cultures (Adams & Carfagna, 2006). Bilingualism, multilingualism and plurilingualism can include any assortment of languages, and the principles of bilingualism are universal. In the case of French, the benefits and opportunities of bilingualism in French include these universal principles, but are framed by the context of French – the unique array of linguistic, cultural, intellectual, and historical contributions of the French language and Francophone culture to the world. The benefits and opportunities of bilingualism in any language are enhanced by the role and status of French as an overall asset.

Bilingualism, the ability to speak more than on language, has personal, professional, and societal benefits. Beyond French borders, the French language exists primarily in bilingual or multilingual environments, in contact with other languages – in other words, in areas where more than one language is used, with the majority of Francophones, or French speakers, located in places where more than one language is

DOI: 10.4324/9781003023760-7

part of their daily lives. Anglophones, or English speakers, are among the least likely to speak additional languages and tend to be reluctant language learners, due in part to a belief that as English is the global *lingua franca*, no other language is needed (Stearns, 2008).

In a globalized and interconnected world, bilingualism is the norm, with more than half of the world population using more than one language on a regular, even daily, basis. For those who may believe that everyone speaks English, the fact is that 75% of the world population does not (British Council, 2013). Multilingualism is a core value of the European Union, and the US does not have an official language. In addition to the personal, cultural, and professional benefits, bilingualism benefits our society by empowering us as more effective global citizens and by building bridges in our increasingly multilingual and multicultural US, where over 60M speak a language other than English at home and where over 2M speak French at home (Ryan, 2013).

Language learning and the use of other languages have been linked to personal benefits, including cultural advantages such as the ability to use another language to better appreciate literature and vocal music, communicative advantages such as the ability to understand news and media reflecting other cultures and worldviews, the relative ease of communicating with others in their language during travel and at home; cognitive and academic benefits including rational thinking, problem-solving, better grades and test scores, and access to information and education in other languages. Multilingualism has also been linked to creativity (Kharkhurin, 2012), and the use of more than one language has been linked to a delay in the onset of symptoms of dementia.

In the workplace, language skills and cultural knowledge have been linked to higher earnings and increased employability, with the demand for bilingual workers rapidly increasing in the US in a wide range of jobs, including not only those in education, health care, and government, language services, and multinational corporations but also those who serve multilingual communities locally, and those that buy and sell products and services beyond US borders (ACTFL, 2019; NAE, 2017). Bilingualism has also been shown to especially benefit low-income children (Hu, 2018). Multilingualism has also been linked to societal benefits including global competitiveness, intercultural understanding and appreciation, and a less segmented society (Daniellson, 2017). It is interesting to note that multilingual countries like Switzerland and Singapore are routinely among the top-ranking nations in the Global Competitiveness Index. On the international level, multilingualism plays a significant role in the development of a global mindset and the values of global citizenship.

Diversity has been linked to creativity and problem-solving, with Leonardo da Vinci perhaps the most high-profile example. However, in day-to-day scenarios, the role of diversity – including linguistic and cultural diversity – is not difficult to envision in settings ranging from high-performance transnational teams to the regional, local, and individual level (Livermore, 2016).

In the US, over 60M speak a language other than English at home. While Spanish is the most frequently spoken language other than English in the US, over 2M speak French (including French Creole) at home, making it the third most widely spoken language (Ryan, 2013). In terms of language learning, 1.3M students are enrolled in French at the K-12 level (American Councils, 2017), and 176K at the college and university level (MLA, 2019), making it the second most widely studied language in the US at both the K-12 and postsecondary levels. The number of Americans with French ancestry is estimated at between 11M and 13M, including French, French-Canadians, Haitians, and people from around the French-speaking world (French-Americans, n.d.).

The US Foreign Language Deficit

However, the US suffers from a foreign language deficit (Stein-Smith, 2013). Not only are relatively few English-speaking Americans able to hold a conversation in another language, but opportunities to learn another language are actually decreasing at all levels, with elementary and middle school programs, as well as college and university programs, decreasing in number and increasingly at risk (AMACAD, 2017; MLA, 2007, 2019).

The challenge is to effectively address this deficit in order to build the language skills and cultural knowledge needed in the workplace, in our society, and as global citizens. Language educators have long advocated for foreign language learning, with advocacy groups at the national, regional, and state levels, and there is a national campaign for language learning, Lead with Languages. In addition, JNCL, an active national lobby for languages, including both organizations of language educators and other language enterprise partners, has an annual National Language Advocacy Day. Support of all these initiatives is clearly indicated, along with increased activity, including a broad coalition of language stakeholders including parents.

With the goals of increasing both language learning and language use, with access available to all, advocacy is a broad umbrella representing a multiplicity of languages, as well as different grade levels and age groups, different methodologies and terminologies, and different uses of language whether within the family, in the school, community, and workplace, or on the global stage as a change agent or researcher.

That being said, the goals of proficiency, authentic use, and access for all are clear, and many voices are needed. Specific areas for advocacy action include an early start to language learning, heritage languages, and public school programs. Although languages can be learned at any age, an early start to language learning is generally linked to successful learning outcomes and to the advocacy goal of proficiency. However, foreign language programs in the elementary schools have decreased in recent years. However, alongside traditional programs, a large number of immersion programs exist, some since the 1970s, but many have come into existence in recent years. Public school programs are especially needed as they offer the broadest access. Support of all initiatives intended to strengthen and support continued language learning beginning at an early age are worthy of support.

Heritage languages are another area directly related to the advocacy goal of proficiency. While heritage learners may possess varying degrees of language skills, many have every likelihood of achieving proficiency, through an early start, and especially where the language is used as a medium of instruction as it is in immersion and where authentic use of the language is likely outside the classroom and beyond the school day. Discussion of heritage languages and heritage language learning, use, and maintenance needs to be informed by the increasing number of heritage language speakers in the US, now well over 60M, and the even greater number of Americans of heritage ancestry whose families at one point spoke a language other than English – now entirely or partially lost through assimilation and other causes.

In both cases, a partnership among language educators, school administrators, parents, and communities is essential in order to develop and sustain public school–based FLES, immersion, and heritage language programs. Examples of successful initiatives include the *revolution bilingue*, where NYC public schools offer immersion programs in about a dozen languages (Jaumont, 2017). At the postsecondary level, college and university programs that have offered interdisciplinary courses and programs, have facilitated double majors and study abroad, and have developed joint programs that include a language component – that have essentially followed the recommendations of the MLA report – have been successful even while other programs have faced challenges (MLA, 2007, 2019).

Challenges to increasing bilingualism and language learning and use, generally, in the US include a reluctance among English-speaking

Americans to learn another language, either fearing that it may be difficult and time-consuming, believing that it is unnecessary, or that English, a global *lingua franca*, is enough. Our own historical and cultural narrative, which tends to highlight the British colonial period and English language rather than considering the American and North American experience from a more holistic perspective, may be another reason for a lack of interest in other languages.

Another challenge is the shortage of foreign language and immersion teachers, due in part to the decline in foreign language majors in recent decades (ACTFL, Educators Rising, n.d.; USDOE, 2021). While there are initiatives to encourage K-12 students to consider a foreign language major and a career in language education, support and advocacy to strengthen existing career pathways to meaningful careers in foreign languages, including but not limited to education, will play a role in building language skills, with qualified teachers needed at all levels and demand for bilingual workers increasing significantly in the US (ACTFL, 2019).

Beyond the teacher shortage, school-based challenges to bilingualism include curricular competition, in which many school subjects compete for the time and attention of students and parents, for funding and support from the local school or school district, and sometimes from relatively more external challenges like coding. While coding is different from a human language in that it is generally not used for interpersonal communication, in literature, or as the means of expression and creativity within one or more cultures, it has, and is, often considered as a substitution for a foreign language requirement – that is, when both are valid skills (Egginton, 2019; Galvin, 2016). Foreign languages, along with the arts, humanities, and social sciences, have also suffered from the increased emphasis on standardized math and English-language reading tests, a legacy of No Child Left Behind, which has at times resulted in a school culture of teaching to the test rather than to the whole child.

The challenges of curricular competition exist also in higher education, where time to degree and the emphasis on preprofessional programs make it more difficult from a scheduling perspective and from a financial perspective for students to opt to continue a language they have already studied and to achieve proficiency or to begin a new language they may be interested in due to the financial, time, and opportunity costs involved. Another challenge revolves around the changes that have taken place in foreign requirements at all levels – for high school graduation, for college entrance, and for college graduation, with waivers and substitutions for a foreign language course that may be perceived as more demanding, real issues at all levels. Double majors, interdisciplinarity, study abroad, joint programs, and online learning are among the approaches that have shown signs of promise, with foreign language the most popular double major in the US (MLA, 2015, 2019).

However, the fact remains that multilingualism is a daily fact of life for approximately half of the world population, who use more than one language on a regular basis, and the US remains largely monolingual in an increasingly multilingual world (Grosjean, 2010, 2020). Language learning and the use of other languages in addition to English are no longer things to be thought of in terms of the future, but are the reality of the interconnected and globalized world and of our increasingly multilingual society (AMACAD, 2020; Montlaur, 2019). Advocacy and partnerships with other language stakeholders play an important role.

How to Develop Multilingualism

As multilingualism brings benefits to the individual, to businesses and other organizations, and to society at the local, national, and global level, it is important to consider how to build language skills and the general language capacity within society – in the classroom, within international organizations, and among the public generally.

The development of a language policy is an important step, as such a policy would bring the question of languages, along with language learning and language use, into the public conversation and would be likely to bring increased resources and funding to support language learning in traditional classrooms and beyond. The language learning environment is another important factor, with an early start to continued language learning and an appropriate level of time devoted to language learning within the school day. Language requirements support language learning, especially when they are specific rather than cafeteria style, and can include both entrance and graduation requirements. Curriculum is another area to consider, with proficiency and communicative language central to the discussion. Authentic language and cultural learning, enhanced by strategic use of technology, is a priority. Traditional foreign language programs beginning at the earliest grade levels, along with immersion programs, need to be supported.

The primary challenge to language learning is motivation, especially in the US and other English-speaking countries, where many may not be aware of the importance of multilingualism generally and/or of the importance of French. On the other hand, motivation has been shown to play a significant role in a successful language learning outcome, and intrinsic motivation – interest in another language and culture, and the desire to learn more – is the strongest motivation in language learning. While this is true of any language, and motivation is a significant factor in language learning outcome, the intrinsic appeal of the French language and Francophone culture can be leveraged to maximize current and potential motivation, along with the opportunities that accompany proficiency in French. Access to literature, the arts, information, and entertainment in French can appeal to many potential French learners to begin studying French and to current French learners to persevere to proficiency and even fluency. As French is one of the top languages in demand in the US and international workplace, opportunities to actually use French language skills and knowledge of Francophone cultures are plentiful, either in terms of French as a requirement for a particular position or in terms of enhancing the resume of the job-seeker. In terms of global citizenship, professional and volunteer positions in any number of global service or nongovernmental organizations (NGOs) are enhanced by a knowledge of French language and Francophone culture.

Specifically in terms of classroom language learning, and although a language can be learned at any age, the earliest possible start is best, as are continued study and a sufficient time dedicated to language study each day or on a regular basis. Traditional foreign language programs in the elementary schools (FLES) are worthy of support, but have diminished in number in recent years, especially in public elementary schools. Immersion programs have been increasing in number in recent years, with parents often playing a significant role in their development and implementation.

In Europe, students typically study one or more additional languages, often including French, from the earliest grade levels, with study abroad programs like Erasmus providing additional learning opportunities. Multilingual education programs, including French and a local language, have been popular in many African countries, especially through the ELAN program. French immersion programs have existed in Canada since the early 1970s, following the enactment of the Official Languages Act, and have proved to be of increasing popularity among parents.

French immersion programs have increased in number in various regions of the US. French immersion programs in Louisiana have existed for more than 50 years, resulting in a "French Renaissance," or rebirth of French and the development of a new generation of Francophones. In February 2021, the France-Louisiana Accords, originally signed in 1968, were renewed, with French immersion programs one of the areas included. The Council for the Development of the French Language in Louisiana (CODOFIL), which celebrated its 50th anniversary in 2018, has played a unique role in French immersion and French language learning, and continues to do so, with new French programs frequently requested by parents. In New York City and beyond, an initiative that has become known as *la Révolution bilingue*, has been associated with the development of immersion programs in a dozen languages, including French, in the New York City public schools. Additional programs exist in other parts of the country as well, with public school implementation important in terms of both enrollment and equity.

French is the second most studied foreign language in the world, especially in Africa and North Africa/the Middle East. French is also the second most popular language in the US at all levels. Unfortunately, however, the number of students enrolled in foreign languages generally has declined at the postsecondary college and university level in the US. French has been the most severely impacted, with nearly 200 programs lost during the most recent reporting period. Challenges to French include the larger context of the crisis of the humanities. French programs have responded to this challenge by developing courses and course sequences in response to student interests and preprofessional plans, and by developing joint programs and double major opportunities.

However, languages exist primarily beyond the classroom, in our homes, communities, our society, and in print, online, and social media. In developing multilingualism, it is necessary to look beyond classroom language learning and to consider language use in our society and in the workplace.

International organizations are among those who have considered the question of language and languages. The United Nations, with over 190 members, has six official languages, one of which is French. French is also one of two working languages of the UN Secretariat. French is one of the official languages of the African Union. The International Olympic Committee has two official languages, one of which is French, which are used along with the local language of the current Olympic venue. In addition, the *Organisation internationale de la Francophonie* (OIF) sends a *Grand Témoin* to ensure that French is used to the appropriate extent at the Olympics. The UN promotes multilingualism through a number of event featuring language and languages throughout the year, and initiatives such as the Many Languages One World Global Youth Forum (MLOW), an initiative of the UN

Academic Impact intended to highlight the role of multilingualism in the development of a global citizenship mindset and values. The European Union considers the primary language of each member state an official language, with French one of three working languages. Multilingualism has been a core value of the European Union, where the majority of adults are able to converse in one additional language, and many are able to use more than one additional language in the workplace. The EU works to promote plurilingualism, or the ability to use more than one language in a variety of community and workplace situations, and even sponsors the European Day of Languages every year in September. The following are just a few examples of how French multilingualism exists beyond French borders.

Languages coexist differently in different countries due to a variety of historical, economic, and societal factors, as does French. Beyond France, while French is often an official or frequently used language, it exists along with other languages and conditions that vary from place to place. Switzerland, Belgium, Luxembourg, and Monaco are examples of French in use beyond France, but in close geographic proximity. In Switzerland, multilingualism is framed and supported by the Languages Act, with the Federal Office of Culture responsible for promoting the four official and national languages French, German, Italian, and Romansch. It is compulsory for all Swiss students to study at least one additional official language, and in recent decades, the number of French language speakers has been increasing. It is considered that Switzerland's linguistic diversity plays a role in its global competitiveness and economic success, it has been calculated that Swiss multilingualism is actually a competitive advantage equal to 10% of the national GDP. Importantly, the role of linguistic diversity and language skills in economic success has led to the realization that investing in foreign languages brings a real economic ROI (return on investment) Federal, n.d.; Wolfestone, n.d.). In his account of growing up bilingual and bicultural, François Grosjean chronicles his linguistic and cultural from France, to Switzerland, to the UK, back to France, then to the US, with a return to Europe in the French-speaking region of Switzerland (Grosjean, 2019). In Belgium, with three official languages, French, Dutch, and German, while there have been language laws, freedom of language continues to be an issue. Luxembourg is a highly multilingual environment, with three administrative languages, French, German, and Luxembourgish, of which French is the main language of communication. Multilingualism is fostered and encouraged through language education in the schools, where students generally learn three foreign languages. French is the official language of Monaco, spoken by over half the population, along with local languages (Languages across Europe, n.d.).

In the Americas, Canada is noteworthy for its Official Languages Act, followed *la Révolution tranquille*/Quiet Revolution, with bilingualism in French and English, along with Québec's *Charter of the French Language*/*La charte de la langue française*, also known as *la Loi*/Bill 101, as well as a half-century tradition of French immersion programs. Challenges include the status of French in Canada beyond Québec, and the status of French generally within Canada highlighted by the use of the official languages in the initial responses to the COVID pandemic. In the US, with no official language but with a long tradition of French and Francophone culture in Louisiana, New England, and other areas, French immersion programs in Louisiana, New York, and other areas have expanded exponentially in recent years. In many African countries, French is an official or widely used language, and multilingual education, educating students in their mother tongue and in French, has been widely embraced. French is also widely spoken in areas of Asia and the Middle East.

Conclusions

Multilingualism is an essential global competency and critical skill in terms of the development of a global mindset and of the values of global citizenship. It is also needed in order to increase understanding and harmony in our increasingly multilingual society (AMACAD, 2020). French is both a global language and a language of the US, and has demonstrated a unique ability to thrive and flourish in multilingual environments around the world.

While cosmopolitanism, or global citizenship, may at first seem an abstract concept, it simply means that the idea that all human beings are, can, and should be citizens in a single worldwide community. In a globalized and interconnected world, the ability to communicate with others in our global community is an essential and a critical skill. In addition, in our own local society, knowledge of heritage languages is not only a way to maintain ties to our own personal cultural identity and to communicate with family members, it is also a way to build and strengthen ties among diverse groups in our society, thereby increasing harmony and reducing segmentation. Language learning and the use of additional languages in our homes and communities, in the workplace, and in our society, are ways in which we can develop the multilingual skills that can enhance our international mindset and facilitate the development of global citizenship values. While the US is a nation of immigrants, remarkably few Americans speak an additional language. Developing interest in and acceptance of the use of other languages is an important first step in developing a comfort level with the idea of a bilingual society, which could be viewed as comfortable bilingualism.

In consideration of the future of multilingualism and of the future of French in the world, it is necessary to highlight the extent to which telecommunications and the relative ease of travel have increased the amount of contact among languages and cultures in an interconnected and globalized world. Historically, geographic proximity played a much more important role in language maintenance, as in the case of francophone Belgium and Switzerland, while today media, travel, and online social media support language learning and maintenance in far-flung locations around the world. In addition to providing a window on another culture, languages can be more easily learned and heritage languages more successfully maintained through travel, study abroad, and widespread access to authentic language and mother tongue speakers.

In addition to providing personal and professional benefits, multilingualism supports diversity and reduces segmentation in society, it also is linked to global competitiveness and economic success, and it is important to stress the economic benefits of multilingualism both in terms of career benefits for the individual and economic benefits for the society as a whole (Hardach, 2018; Hogan-Brun, 2017). While international organizations, nations, and regions have approached multilingualism differently, the development of a language policy is an initial step to create a framework for sustainable multilingualism. French is a unique example of a language that exists primarily within multilingual environments, and local efforts to support French language learning and the maintenance of French as a heritage global language are supplemented by the current worldwide campaign for French as a global language. This campaign, supported by the French government is framed by the three pillars of learning, communication, and creativity, which frame 21st-century skills, of which multilingualism may arguably be the most important, just as it provides the means through which the UN Sustainable Development Goals can only be realized through goal 17, the partnership for the goals.

7 French Language Learning in the US

Introduction

As the second most widely studied language in the US (American Councils, 2017), there is strong interest in French language learning across the country, whether through traditional foreign language programs or through immersion. There are also more than 10M Americans of French ancestry who have varying levels of knowledge of the French language. In addition, there are more French nationals making their homes in the US in recent years as well as numerous immigrants from Francophone regions around the world. In addition to individual learning needs and learning decisions, each of these groups may have different goals and priorities in terms of French language learning and use.

As far as classroom learning is concerned, the availability of foreign language learning, including French, for all interested students is not a given, with the percentage of schools offering foreign languages in the elementary and middle school level declining. This is especially disturbing as an early start to learning offers not only the opportunity to maximize the potential present among children to learn other languages but also a longer number of years for continued study of a language, another factor in achieving proficiency. Postsecondary programs in colleges and universities in foreign languages, including French, have also declined in recent years, resulting in fewer opportunities for students to learn preprofessional language skills which would enhance the possibility of maximizing the benefit of language skills as a career asset.

Reflecting the historical French presence in what is now the US, Americans of French ancestry are found throughout the country, with large numbers of Franco-Americans primarily of French-Canadian and Acadian descent in New England and many of Acadian and Creole

DOI: 10.4324/9781003023760-8

heritage in Louisiana. South Florida is home to the fastest-growing Francophone community, largely of Haitian descent, and recent arrivals from France can be found in New York, San Francisco, and beyond. With 80K Francophones, New York City has been described as the Francophone capital of the US (Sicot & Brunet, 2020).

While heritage learners share many characteristics of classroom learners, in addition to varying levels of language knowledge, they may have a wide range of interests and backgrounds, and be of any age. For this reason, a classroom-like setting, or one-size-fits-all community events may not be effective (Tropea, 2018). Those who speak French may also speak differing regional varieties of French, which can add an additional dimension to French language learning and use.

Immigrants and new arrivals to the US form a subset of heritage speakers with their own priorities and learning needs. Within this group, there are often mother tongue language skills, but younger family members, especially those born in the US, may speak the language to varying degrees and may have different levels of reading and writing skills. For families, in addition to being an educational question, it is a question of culture and identity, with language change making it difficult or impossible for younger family members to communicate effectively, or at all, with older relatives. For this group, French immersion programs, with their use of French as a medium of instruction rather than as a foreign language or mere school subject, may be especially attractive.

Languages, however, exist as an integral part of life, within the classroom, but also beyond – before and after the school day, outside of school, and in adult and professional life when school is largely left behind. In order for a language to flourish, or even to survive, it needs to be part of the social fabric of the home and community, an means of communication used in authentic contexts, a source of information and entertainment, and part of the creative sphere, either as a creative participant or as an appreciative observer.

Lastly, the French language and Francophone cultural community includes all those who admire French language and Francophone culture, often referred to as Francophiles, who are current and potential participants in French language learning and use initiatives. Although learning the language provides wonderful access to another culture, Francophiles – who often also speak French to varying degrees – can be wonderful allies in developing community, cultural, and creative events featuring French language and Francophone culture and opportunities for all to use the language and for students and young people to develop preprofessional skills and to access career opportunities enhanced by their ability to use French in a business setting.

The Status of French Language Learning in the US

French is the second most widely studied language in the US, both at the K-12 and college and university level, with 1.3 million students enrolled in French at the elementary and high school level, and 176,000 at the college and university level – declining at the postsecondary level (American Councils, 2017; MLA, 2019).

In the US, French teachers are represented by the AATF (American Association of Teachers of French), which has close to 10,000 members, state and regional chapters, and national commissions, as well as sponsoring awards, contests, and events, including National French Week. In addition, many French language educators participate in national, regional, and state foreign language education associations (AATF, 2019).

The role of technology in language learning, already an important aspect, has been highlighted by the COVID-19 pandemic, which has greatly expanded distance/remote virtual online learning. Various US publishers offer K-12 and college textbooks and online learning platforms for the beginning and intermediate levels of French language learning.

Although a language can be learned at any time in life, if continued language study begins at an early age, the child's natural abilities and the length of time for continued study, favor a successful learning outcome, and the two types of language instruction commonly available are traditional foreign language learning (FLES), and immersion (which has several models) in which – rather than being a school subject to be learned – the language is the medium of instruction, or tool for learning. Intercomprehension, more frequently discussed in the European context, and reflecting relative ease with which speakers of closely related languages and understanding each other's written and spoken language, could provide additional pathways for the many speakers of other Romance languages, including Spanish, in the US in acquiring French language skills. Programs and curriculum that respond to the needs of Romance language speakers, especially the many Spanish speakers in the US, maximize their ability to understand French, and specifically teach strategies to facilitate this comprehension should be a top priority for French language stakeholders, supporters, and advocates.

One of the most noteworthy trends in French language learning is the popularity of French immersion programs, driven in part by the increase in the number of French and Francophone families living in the US and desirous of maintaining the French language in addition to English. While immersion programs exist for various languages, the French example is particularly interesting because of the active involvement of the French government, through the French dual-language immersion fund launched during the September 2017 visit of then-newly elected French President Macron to New York City to address the United Nations as he spoke at the CUNY graduate center. These funds are intended to be used primarily not only for the development of curriculum materials but also to support immersion teacher training. Anchorage, Alaska, is among the most recent French immersion programs. Whether French is learned in a traditional foreign language class setting or through immersion, an early start is of the utmost important, and parents are the most important stakeholders and supporters.

Additional opportunities for French language learning exist through various intensive bootcamp-style immersion programs, the best known of which include Middlebury College and Concordia Language Villages. Preprofessional French language skills are highlighted in programs at the University of Wisconsin and in French Chamber of Commerce initiatives to provide faculty training and education. French job fairs incentivize the acquisition of French language skills for professional purposes. Adult learners may be served through traditional institutions, most notably community colleges, through workplace learning programs, and through language schools, including online services.

Issues in French language education in US schools and colleges include curriculum, choice of textbook/online learning platform, opportunities for conversation, practice, and exposure to authentic language, etc. Challenges include the fact that foreign languages, including French, are elective courses.

However, language as a means of communication and self-expressions transcends the classroom, and in order for a language to thrive, it must be used in authentic settings in order to be sustainable. In the case of French, there are two aspects to this concept, *francoresponsabilité*, which refers to the responsibility of the linguistic community to maintain and encourage use of the language in a variety of authentic settings, and *francodurabilité*, or sustainable learning and use of the French language (CODOFIL, 2021).

Governments – in France and in the US – are both stakeholders and supporters of the French language. Through the dual-language French immersion initiative, the French-American Cultural Exchange

(FACE) Foundation, and other initiatives, along with the presence of the French cultural counselor, educational attaches, the *Alliance Française*, and programs to support French language education and educators in the US, the French government works to support French language and Francophone culture in the US and throughout the world. The *Alliance Française* in Portland, Maine, is among the most recent to open in the US. Among US governments, Louisiana has joined the *Organisation internationale de la Francophonie* (OIF), establishing a cultural and business relationship with over 80 Francophone member regions/nations.

Additional Opportunities for French Education in the US

However, in addition to traditional and immersion French language programs in public, charter, and private US schools, the French language learning environment in the US includes the *Alliance Française*, independent schools, French schools, and French heritage programs.

French schools have existed in the US since the earliest years of our history, with the Lycée Français de New York perhaps the best known in the country. Founded in the 1930s, it is an independent school receiving no funding from the French government, accredited by both New York State and the French Ministry of Education, and offers a French and American curriculum leading to both a French baccalaureate and an American high school diploma (Ross, 2020). Opportunities for a French education in the US also include the nearly 50 elementary and secondary schools that are part of the Association of French Schools in America (AFSA). These schools are accredited by the French Ministry of Education and offer a French curriculum accompanied by some North American elements (AFSA, n.d.). A strength of these schools is the combination of immersion education in French, along with the development of both a French and global identity.

Created in 2005, with the goal of helping underserved Francophone students to maximize the role of French in their personal and professional futures, the French Heritage Language Programs are an initiative of the FACE Foundation and the French Embassy in the US and serves students New York City, Boston, Maine, and Massachusetts. Other noteworthy educational programs include Community College in France, intended to enable first-generation US community college students to study in France and the Thomas Jefferson Fund, which supports young researchers.

There are also possibilities for French language and Francophone cultural learning beyond the traditional educational institutions.

Among these, perhaps the best-known setting for French language learning around the world is the *Alliance Française*. With over 800 chapters worldwide of which over 100 are in the US, the *Alliance Française* offers language learning opportunities, cultural events, and more, in collaboration with the *Institut Français*.

The Importance of Leadership, Advocacy, and Social Movements

Within the context of a decline in foreign language programs at the elementary and middle school level, and the fact the French has been the most severely impacted at the postsecondary level in recent years, this is the time for leadership among French language educators, advocates, and supporters. Leadership has been described as "a process whereby an individual influences a group of individuals to achieve a common goal" (Northouse, 2013), and these elements of process, influence, groups, and common goals are key to the leadership needed on the part of foreign language stakeholders to bring about a resurgence of interest in foreign languages and in French among US learners and decision-makers. This is an opportunity for all those who believe in French as a personal asset, 21st-century skill, and as a social and economic benefit, to advocate for the French language in the US within the broader framework of foreign languages in the US and of multilingualism as a global competency.

In addition to the need for leadership and leaders, advocacy is of critical importance in moving the agenda forward in terms of bringing about the resurgence of French within the context of a multilingual revolution in the US. Advocacy has been described as "persuading people who matter to care about your issue" (Daly, 2011). It means bringing to the table new ideas that may involve change, and overcoming obstacles in terms of philosophy and belief, but also in terms of resources, logistics, and funding. It may even mean stopping a bad idea, or a decision to cut or eliminate a French program, that is already on the table, under discussion, or almost decided. Most importantly, advocacy is about empowerment. Advocacy methods can effectively utilize strategies and tactics from public relations, marketing, social marketing, change management, the psychology of persuasion, blue ocean strategy, disruptive innovation, negotiation, lobbying, confrontation, and more. While advocacy may include support of national and regional campaigns in support of French, advocacy is a broad umbrella, and many voices are needed. As far as methods are concerned, every concerned believer may use whatever methods may be available within the available skills set and funding of the individual or group.

In essence, the resurgence of French language and Francophone culture is a social movement, and as such, is characterized by the idea of individuals and small groups united in a shared purpose, in this case, French in the US and beyond (Satell & Popovic, 2017). As leaders and advocates within a social movement for French, it is important to clearly define the desired change, aka that French reassume its true place in our American culture and identity, to attract allies through the appeal of French, aka, through soft power and influence, and to develop a sustainable plan for French.

Moving forward, French language stakeholders need to build awareness of the importance of awareness, knowledge, and the implementation of any and all of the methods likely to foster a reawakening of interest in learning and using French and in engaging with Francophone culture. Training in leadership, advocacy, and social movements, whether in the classroom, on the job, or through professional associations and mentoring, is essential in order to develop the leadership and advocacy and political skills needed to effect social change.

Conclusions

The *atout* or advantage of French in the marketplace of ideas lies in the appeal of its culture, lifestyle, and ideas. Whether it is the desirability of travel or study abroad, a global lifestyle, or the great humanistic ideas of the Renaissance and the Founding Fathers through to the present day. Above all, it is essential for all French language stakeholders to maximize the appeal of French culture as a gateway to language learning and cultural knowledge, understanding, and appreciation, ranging from discussions of ideas past and present to the current popular culture and the global success of the TV series *Lupin*.

8 The French Language and Francophone Culture in the US
French as a Heritage Language and Global Competency

Introduction

French language and Francophone culture are present on the five continents, and the French presence in what is now the US dates from the earliest years of European exploration. French is a global language in business and international organizations, and the *Organisation internationale de la Francophonie* (OIF) includes nearly 90 member nations and regions, including the US state of Louisiana. Part of our US cultural identity, French place names in the US ranging from Coeur d'Alene to Detroit and New Orleans, and French family names of famous Americans including Jack Kerouac, Jacqueline Bouvier Kennedy, and Timothée Chalamet, highlight our French heritage. Public figures, including Secretaries of State John Kerry and Antony Blinken, and celebrities like Bradley Cooper and Jodie Foster, are fluent in French. More French nationals are making their home in the US, and new Americans number many from throughout the Francophone world. French is everywhere in American daily life, from *macarons* and cronuts, to the television series *Lupin*.

While some Americans may believe that English is enough, and that English is the global *lingua franca*, spoken by all, this is not the case. English is not enough, it is spoken by only one quarter of the world population, and we live in a multilingual world, where at least half the world population regularly uses more than one language (AMACAD, 2017, 2020; British Council, 2013).

The US is at a turning point in terms of French as a heritage language and French language skills and knowledge of Francophone culture as a global competency in the US. Not only is French a global language, spoken around the world, but it is also an American language, spoken by over 2M at home in the US and part of the heritage and cultural identity of over 10M Americans. The challenge is to

DOI: 10.4324/9781003023760-9

foster French language learning and knowledge of Francophone culture within the context of global citizenship, and also as part of our US cultural identity.

This challenge needs to be considered within the context of global competencies, international education, and foreign language learning. It also needs to take into consideration the opportunities for use of a second language, in this case French, in our homes, communities, and the workplace. While many Anglophones may consider English, a global *lingua franca*, sufficient, the reality is that three-quarters of the world population does not speak English, and English is not sufficient in the present and moving forward (AMACAD, 2017, 2020).

The Current Status of French in the US

In order to bring about a resurgence of French language and Francophone culture in the US, it is important to look at French language learning, but also at the use of French and the interest in Francophone culture beyond the classroom. In terms of French language learning, an early start to continued learning is one of the best predictors of a successful learning outcome, so early childhood and elementary/middle school programs should be supported and strengthened, and new ones developed and implemented whenever possible. Sadly, elementary and middle school programs have declined in recent years (AMACAD, 2017), and public elementary programs in foreign languages are not available to the majority of students, including those lower-income students who are the most likely to benefit from bilingualism. There is of great interest in immersion programs, but it is important that these programs be available to all interested students through public schools rather than in private settings, or only in limited geographic areas and school districts. In the short term, parents and other language stakeholders, including community leaders and interested educators, should certainly work together in a collaborative partnership to create and implement these programs, but a longer-term strategy including career pathways and interest in the broader community and in the media are key to bringing French into our daily lives. Despite the fact that many aspects of public education are governed at the state and local level, a US foreign language policy supporting multilingualism would go a long way toward ensuring both interest in other languages and the potential funding critical to sustainable language programs.

At the college and university level, the current decline in enrollments has resulted in the elimination and closure of many programs, and French has been the language most severely impacted at this time.

At the postsecondary level, therefore, a different two-pronged strategy is needed to strengthen and support at-risk programs immediately in order to avoid the loss of even more programs, but also to develop longer-term solutions in order to effectively address the decline in interest and in enrollment in order to develop sustainable French language learning moving forward. French language educators, advocates, and stakeholders need to work together collaboratively to create courses and career pathways to appeal to a wide variety of student personal and professional interests, to develop interdisciplinary collaborations and joint programs in order to both respond to student needs and to strengthen support for French and for languages generally across the campus. Double majors, already a popular choice among students interested both in foreign languages and in another discipline, need to be encouraged and facilitated administratively.

However, the ongoing challenge resides in the relatively small number of US students who study languages at the K-12 level – fewer than 20% (American Councils, 2017), which results in an insufficient number of students at the university level with the skills needed to effectively engage in preprofessional learning. In order to reverse this insufficient marketing funnel and to develop sustainable foreign language programs at the college and university level, it is necessary to increase the number of K-12 foreign language learners, especially in the earliest grade levels, in order to have a sufficient number of college students with both the motivation and skills needed to develop preprofessional proficiency at the college and university level.

The growing interest in immersion programs is an area of special interest to French language educators, advocates, and stakeholders. Ensuring that these highly sought-after programs are available to all interest students is a top priority. In addition, ensuring curriculum continuity beyond elementary school is essential, allowing middle and high school students can continue to grow in terms of language proficiency and cultural skills so that the number of students interested and skilled in French at the college level reached the number needed for sustainable French programs.

French Language Advocacy

With already declining enrollments in French exacerbated by the global COVID-19 pandemic, advocacy is more necessary than ever before – in order to create not only sustainable French language learning but also sustainable use of French in our communities, in the workplace, in the media, and in our society as a whole.

Career pathways need to be developed in the French curriculum in our schools and colleges, and partnerships with global Francophone organizations and businesses need to be developed in order to encourage careers using French through internships and recruitment. In addition, creativity needs to be encouraged, in terms of opportunities for creative activity across the disciplines in French, and using French and Francophone ideas, and based on French and Francophone core values.

Advocacy needs to be smart and strategic, maximizing the effect, or ROI (return on investment) of the limited time and resources available to busy teachers after all their classroom and professional obligations are completed. Advocacy is also for everyone, for all who care about the *rayonnement* of French language and Francophone culture, and each individual can choose whichever area is most of interest – curriculum, careers, culture, methodology, etc. Advocacy also needs to take advantage of all the opportunities and technologies freely available to get the message out to the community. In addition to advocacy by educators, however, advocacy for French language and Francophone culture transcends the classroom and envision goals that encompass the whole of society.

While French language educators have been well organized through their professional associations at the state, regional, and national level and have advocated with dedication and professionalism for decades, making known the personal and professional benefits of French language knowledge and cultural skills, enrollment has declined at the college and university level, and foreign language programs have declined at the elementary and middle school level. Still the second most studied foreign language in the US, French, has suffered the most dramatic impact in terms of college and university programs lost in recent years.

Advocacy is needed more than ever, in order to avoid additional program losses now and in order to build a sustainable French language learning framework K-16, beginning at the earliest grade levels, through undergraduate and graduate programs. In addition, it is necessary to support immersion programs, best positioned to develop language skills and cultural understanding within an authentic environment and from an early age. Collaborations between elementary, middle school, and high school educators is essential in developing and maintaining interest in French, as well as smooth transitions in continued learning and a foundation in the use of French in the workplace and in creative projects. Collaborations between K-12 and college and university educators share similar goals, with preprofessional and global citizenship uses of French playing a larger role at the postsecondary level. In immediate terms, programs at the elementary and middle school levels need to be strengthened and supported, and new ones created, while at the college and university levels, there is an urgent need to develop multidisciplinary collaborations in order to allow for double majors, joint programs, and preprofessional curricula to respond to student interests.

Advocacy lies in developing sustained interest and motivation, through a realization of the empowerment that comes from speaking a global language and of the joy of being able to communicate with a worldwide culture renowned for its achievements, beauty, and creativity. Personal and Professional Empowerment

Any discussion of advocacy requires consideration of the rationale, or reason why advocacy is needed, as well as of the methods of advocacy. Multilingualism generally is a personal, professional, and social/societal benefit or advantage, empowering those who can communicate effectively with others in their languages. In the case of French, a global language, the empowerment of the person who has acquired French as a learned second language is evident. The methods of advocacy, while variable according to local circumstances, include promoting both the learning and use of French through all available means – in person and online, using persuasion, change management, social marketing, negotiation, confrontation, lobbying, etc., through professional engagement, speaking, research, writing, and through political and social action.

While French is a global language of culture and business, of communication, learning, and creativity and innovation, most French speakers live in a multilingual context, and therefore, in an environment where languages are in contact, in a fluid and dynamic environment where language gain or lose influence depending on a variety of factors. For this reason, it is especially important for French language speakers and stakeholders remain vigilant and even proactive in terms of advocacy and promotion for French language and Francophone culture.

In light of the global role of French in many multilingual environments, the French government, in 2018, launched a campaign for the promotion of French, on the occasion of the Journee internationale de la Francophonie on March 20th, announced by French President Macron (Chrisafis, 2018). This campaign, with 33 objectives based on the pillars of learning, communication, and creativity, followed a period of gathering ideas on French from informants around the world and led by personal representative of the President (France Diplomacy, International Strategy, n.d.). While local institutions and initiatives exist around the world to defend and promote the learning and use of French, this French government campaign can provide direction and focus to otherwise disparate efforts, at the same time recognizing that local histories and situations require local participation and involve local issues (France Diplomacy, Francophony, n.d.).

In the US, challenges to French include the general reluctance of English speakers, who believe that English is the global *lingua franca* and that any additional languages are unnecessary. Although this belief is erroneous, and only 25% of the world population speaks English (British Council, 2013), this misconception – along with the "melting pot" metaphor that predominated in the US well into the 20th century – led to both the loss of many heritage languages in the US and to a general lack of interest in learning new languages among English-speaking Americans. Another challenge is the lack of access to continued foreign language learning, with the relatively few foreign language programs at the elementary and middle school level declining in number, along with those in colleges and universities, with French the most severely impacted (MLA, 2019). Despite the stature of French as a global language, as a language of culture, diplomacy, and business, and despite the long-standing presence of French language and Francophone culture in the US, advocacy is needed, and it is necessary to think about the role and nature of advocacy and about the steps needed to restore French to its rightful place in the US.

Advocacy can be defined as "persuading people who matter to care about your issue." In terms of specific action steps, "it is about getting listened to, being at the table when decisions are made, being heard by people who make decisions." Winning over decision-makers and influencers is at the heart of advocacy, and persuasion and lobbying are the means. However, it is also "about facing and overcoming resistance," making negotiation and even confrontation tools of the advocate. For the influencer, the scholar, and the public intellectual, "it is about speaking and writing in compelling ways that make decision makers want to adopt your ideas," bringing online and social media, blogs, opinion pieces and research articles, and conference presentations tools of advocacy (Daly, 2011).

However, these advocacy tools and skills, and even an advocacy mindset, are not necessarily part of the background, education, training, or temperament of every French-language stakeholder, or of everyone who cares about French language and Francophone culture and its future in the US.

The first step in change management is to create "a sense of urgency" (Kotter, 2008). The urgency in French language advocacy is real despite the global importance of French globally and its significance as an American language. If the pipeline of learners diminishes, as is currently happening, the future of French is bleak. If those students who are actually in French programs do not see opportunities to use French in the workplace and in their daily lives, the future of French is bleak. The psychology of persuasion rests on the ability to connect in a positive with the other, an essential skill for the French language advocate (Cialdini, 20). It is essential to connect with local communities and beyond, from the classroom to the board room, to persuade others of the immense value of French language skills and Francophone cultural knowledge. Advocacy for French rests on a foundation of personal, professional, and social/societal empowerment, and social marketing, or the use of marketing strategies and tactics, for the greater good (Lee & Kotler, 2015). It is essential to base advocacy for French in the empowerment that it brings to all who learn it and use it both locally and globally, but also in the boost that it gives to each learner's ability to act for the greater good.

Advocacy is both a mindset and a skills set. On the one hand, in order to be effective, advocacy needs to be values-driven – with belief and conviction in the necessity of multilingualism as a personal and professional asset, and as an advantage to our society and to our world part of the core values of the French language stakeholder, supporter, and advocate. Advocacy is also data-driven, and part of the skills set of the French language stakeholder, whether educator, heritage speaker, language enterprise stakeholder, or Francophile. Data and information, abundant on both the importance of multilingualism and on the significance of French in all areas of life, are essential in effectively "making the case" for French language learning and use. While advocacy takes place within professional associations and by smaller groups and individuals, the elements of advocacy include a panoply of methods from the worlds of business and politics, including change management, social marketing, the psychology of persuasion, negotiation, and lobbying, to name just a few. Advocacy also takes place every day and in emergency situations, such as when the implementation of a French program is rejected, or a French program is at risk. Advocacy takes place in person, online, and in research, writing, and speaking.

Use of the French Language beyond the Classroom

Despite the challenges facing French programs, especially those in elementary and middle schools, and those in colleges and universities, it is important to remember that French, like any language, is part of the whole of life, within the classroom, and beyond. French language supporters and advocates need to work to ensure that French language and Francophone culture are part of daily life in our homes and communities, in the workplace, and in the media and the public conversation. In alignment with the pillars of the French government campaign to promote French worldwide, learning, communication, and creativity form the pathway to the resurgence of French in the US and to its promotion worldwide. In addition to providing opportunities for all our children to learn other languages, including French, in our schools, we need opportunities for the use of French in daily life.

The use of an additional language and the adoption of its values is a social movement impacting all segments of society, while at the same time reducing segmentation through shared multilingualism. Advocacy for the learning and use of French needs to adopt the mindset and methods of political action and social movements.

Like social movements generally, which include "small groups that are loosely connected but united by a shared purpose," advocacy for French is a sustained grass-roots movement to bring about social change through collective action, in this case, a greater acceptance of Francophone culture as part of the global and local culture and an increased use of French across all sectors of society (Satell & Popovic, 2017).

With over 2M speaking French at home and well over 10M of French ancestry in the US, not to mention many more Francophiles and other language supporters, enthusiasts, and advocates, there is potential for the level of commitment and engagement needed to bring about social change. However, as these many individuals and groups remain not only separate, but even unknown to one another, the challenge remains to create that sense of shared purpose. While social media can play an important role in bringing together disparate and far-flung individuals and groups, a sustained dialogue and a desire to work together in a shared purpose are needed, and thought leaders and influencers across the country and representing various interest groups can play a significant role in moving the initiative forward.

In the case of the US, advocacy for the French language and Francophone culture should be inclusive, including educators and educational institutions, but also parents, communities, heritage language and cultural groups, and language supporters in government and business, as well as external elements such as the French government, OIF, and the *Centre de la Francophonie des Amériques* (CFA), in addition to local and regional groups like the Franco-American Centre of New Hampshire (FACNH).

Conclusions

While the need for multilingualism is better known and more widely accepted in the US, and French is more present than ever in the lives of

Americans, language acquisition and language maintenance are long-term processes requiring time and support. In order to bring about a resurgence of French in the US, it is important that accessibility to language learning generally be available to all students, and that language learning and use of other languages be fostered and encouraged in education, the workplace, and in our society and media. A US language policy encouraging language acquisition and use, as well as the maintenance of heritage languages is needed. As far as French is concerned, bringing together the many French voices present in the US in support of a shared goal of building French bilingualism/Francophonie among Americans will have the greatest impact on the future of French in the US.

Current Trends and Future Directions for the French Language in the US

Reflecting the global appeal of French culture and lifestyle, and of the French language, French is the second most widely studied additional language in the US, as it is in the world. It is a global language of culture, education, business, information, diplomacy, and global citizenship. It is also a language spoken by millions of Americans of French heritage, by the newest Americans, and by countless American Francophiles. It is also increasingly a language to which Americans increasingly turn for media and entertainment, with TV5Monde alone reaching 1.5 million US viewers every week (TV5Monde: Who Are We?, 2021) and over 300 French books translated into English each year (Cultural Services, 2021). It is no coincidence that *Lupin*, a French-language show, has been the most successful non-English language Netflix offering. Moving forward, it is essential that French-language stakeholders reexamine, rethink, and reimagine the role of French in our lives – past, present, and future.

French is everywhere – as close as a visit to Québec, Louisiana, or New York, in our history and heritage, and in our personal and professional lives. However, French transcends the individual. The French presence, or *espace Francophone*, is *global et mondial*, impacts every aspect of our lives, wherever we may be – all day, every day. In our personal lives, in terms of culture and travel, in terms of our careers and employment in the global workplace and as members of transnational teams, in terms of our commitment or *engagement* as cosmopolitan and global citizens, and in terms of our ability to build relationships both local and global, French is part of our lives. At present, more than 10M Americans claim French ancestry, and more than 2M Americans speak French at home. The challenge – or *défi* or *enjeu* – is to develop an environment for sustainable French language learning and use in the US. We can – and should – wake up every morning determined to make French part of our lives, speaking and using French as part of our daily routine and working together to ensure that all our children have the opportunity to learn additional languages and that the value of French as a language in our communities, in our society, and in our lives as global citizens is effectively communicated and supported.

The true appeal of French lies in its role as a world language and its ability to support and sustain connections in the workplace, in our communities, and in the globalized world. Leveraging these real-world roles of French in our lives and centering French language learning on authentic language and experience and on its communicative role in building relationships between individuals and communities are an essential step in making the use of French part of our daily lives. Face-to-face and virtual encounters with mother tongue speakers from throughout the *Francophonie*, and access to music, media, entertainment, and popular fiction as a complement to more traditional curriculum will enhance both cultural understanding and language skills.

For these reasons, it is essential that all of those interested in learning and using French in their daily lives have access to a wide range of inputs, or sources of authentic language and culture. Textbooks and online learning platforms, along with media intended to be viewed by non-mother-tongue speakers, certainly serve a purpose and have a place, especially at the beginning levels. However, just as the learning and use of a language, in this case French, transcend any specific discipline or school subject, and go beyond the classroom albeit face-to-face or virtual, being rather a quintessentially interdisciplinary part of life, language has to be used in a variety of authentic settings. While French language and Francophone culture are well represented in all areas of culture, the arts, education, information, and business, 21st-century technologies have made it exponentially easier for most to access elements of the popular culture and daily uses of the language that in earlier eras were available only to those who could afford extensive stays in France.

Those interested in bringing French home from the classrooms into their daily lives continue to have even easier access to classic French film, but also have access to new reports, interviews and talk shows, cooking and home improvement shows, along with comedy and drama series. It is also important to distinguish between French media developed primarily for an international audience versus movies, TV shows, and online media developed as entertainment or information for a home market, with those intended for local access possibly offering better insight for the external learner or Francophile. While

French literature holds a unique position in literary studies and appreciation, French magazines and newspapers, once challenging to obtain in a timely manner in major US cities, are now readily available in real time at little or no cost online. French books, both classic literature and popular fiction and nonfiction, are readily available either as ebooks or through online vendors.

Just as French language learning and use are complementary yet separate concepts, so too are the environments and dynamics of each. French language learning can be viewed through different perspectives or lenses, those of grade level, of methodology, of intensity, and also of in-person, virtual, hybrid, immersion, boot camp, study abroad or study away, and whether the goal is language skill and intercultural communication versus learning about the language and culture, and whether the learner is within and institution or a self-directed independent learner. Each of these modalities has advantages and disadvantages. Language use is similar in that it has various pathways, but it is different in that it has a tangible, visible, societal goal.

In order to develop a sustainable French presence/*espace Francophone* in the US, it is necessary to raise the profile of French and motivation to learn and use French in our society, and at the same time, to expand opportunities for foreign language learning and use – including French – in our media and in our society, and many hands and voices are needed. Support for French language learning and use in the US involves, therefore, not only French language educators and their institutions but also French-speaking communities in the US, Francophiles, and language enterprise partners in business and government.

There are more and more French-speaking, or Francophone, Americans, including not only heritage speakers, Franco-Americans who may have a long-standing cultural identity of several centuries in North America and in the US but also the newest Americans – French nationals and recent arrivals from throughout the French-speaking world. While one often thinks of New England and Louisiana in terms of French language and Francophone culture, there are vibrant communities of French language stakeholders throughout the US.

With 10M Americans of French heritage and 2M who speak French at home, the future of French looks promising – if we ensure that all interested students have the opportunity to begin continued study of French at an early age, and if we provide pathways to preprofessional skills and opportunities for authentic use of French in the workplace and in our society. In both the North American context and a globalized world, the future of French transcends the historical Franco-American *survivance* to become a sustainable part of US culture.

As the US becomes increasingly multilingual, with over 60M speaking a language other than English at home, the mindset toward learning and use of other languages in addition to English may be changing – and communities across the country are clamoring for immersion language programs, leading an increasing number of public and political persons to support these initiatives. While the importance of the presence and impact of France, the French language, and French/Francophone culture on our heritage and our contemporary culture is undeniable, their importance continues to grow within the US. The growing importance is highlighted not only in the form of increasing numbers of Francophones from France, Haiti, Africa, and the French-speaking world making their home throughout the US, but also of an increasingly interconnected globalized world bringing French and Francophone business and media to the US.

However, the resurgence of French is also attributable to efforts of Franco-Americans – whether descendants of the earliest French explorers and settlers, of French Canadian immigrants throughout our history, or of the most recent arrivals from Haiti, Africa, and the French-speaking world, working to make better known their story and their remarkable contribution to the US.

While language skills vary widely among any heritage language community, ranging from mother tongue fluency to little or no linguistic knowledge, it is important to remember that over 10M in the US are of French ancestry, and French remains the second most widely studied language in the US. Interest in language learning has resulted in a sharp rise in the number of French language immersion programs and French heritage language programs throughout the country (Cultural Services, n.d.). The next step is the promotion of use of French beyond the classroom – in the community, in the workplace, and in our society.

It is also interesting to note that Louisiana joined the OIF in 2018, after 50 years of French language promotion through immersion education and a current campaign to promote the business use of French (France Diplomacy, Francophony, n.d.). The fastest growing Francophone community in the US is in Florida, the growth of French language learning and use driven not only by French expatriates and French Canadian tourists but also by a growing Haitian community where French Creole is spoken.

Conclusions – The Future of French – The French Language
Past, Present, and Future

Closing the loop, the time to act is now. The use of French needs to be part of our daily lives – the time for resolutions and good intentions has passed; French needs to become a habit, part of the fabric of our regular routine, used automatically in a wide range of situations and settings.

At present, French media, entertainment, ideas, and lifestyle are sought after and emulated around the world and in the US. The current unprecedented popularity of French TV series like *Lupin* and *Call My Agent*, along with French-themed series like *Emily in Paris*, is just an example of the *attractivité* of French and Francophone culture. French is the second most studied language around the world and in the US, and Paris is the most popular destination for international visitors. People around the world and in the US are interested in, engaged with, and excited about the French language and Francophone culture, possibly more than at any time in recent years. While the current status of French is wonderful, a challenge is how to bridge the gap between interest in the culture and language learning, particularly among Americans who are among the most reluctant language learners. The gap between those who use the French language and those who are interested in the history, literature, lifestyle, and culture in translation – viewed through the lens of their mother tongue – is considerable, and in the US and among English speakers especially, is considerable, and shows no signs of narrowing or closing any time soon. This paradoxical situation – of significant interest in a culture without the accompanying understanding of its language, its primary vehicle of communication, education, and creativity – often goes virtually unnoticed.

The reasons for this gap are many, ranging from lack of interest in language learning among many Americans to lack of opportunity for language learning and a shortage of qualified teachers.

DOI: 10.4324/9781003023760-10

Conclusions – The Future of French

The question then arises as to how to address this gap between the significant number of Americans who are interested in French language and Francophone culture, often referred to as Francophiles, who have varying degrees of linguistic skills and cultural knowledge, and the more than 10M in the US of French heritage, who may have varying backgrounds, cultural knowledge, language skills, and interest. In addition, the more than 2M in the US who speak French at home, many of whom are recent immigrants to the US, are also potential partners and French language stakeholders and supporters.

Building the Francophone Community

This diverse community of those who are already interested in French language and Francophone culture to widely varying degrees, along with those who have French heritage as part of their family story and personal cultural identity – and these may be overlapping sectors – is both an opportunity and a challenge. The sheer number of people in the US alone with a family or affectionate connection to French language and culture, and those whose interest and/or skills may lie dormant awaiting only the right set of circumstances to be reawakened presents a significant opportunity for French language advocates. On the other hand, the wide range of interests along with the possibly even wider range of French language skills – from nonexistent to fluent, near-native, and native speakers – presents challenges for those who would wish to develop and implement a strategic plan to strengthen and promote French language and Francophone culture in the US.

This first aspect, designing events intended to answer the interests of participants of different ages and personal interests, resembles the challenges facing those planning programs, activities, and events everywhere, and events can be envisioned accordingly. However, it is the difference in language skills that poses a more unique, and difficult, challenge for the planner. While it is not difficult to imagine events in English, or in French, planning bilingual events, activities, and programs of interest to participants with different skill levels is much more difficult to envision and to implement. This is even more the case when the desire is not merely to provide a translation for the English speaker, but rather to encourage the learning and use of French in authentic settings and situations and to facilitate the transition from English to French.

The planning of a bilingual event rests in making everyone – those who are bilingual and those who only may speak one of the languages – feel equally comfortable and engaged, and it is important to try to

Conclusions – The Future of French

determine the audience as early as possible in the planning process and to plan the content of the event accordingly in order to meet the needs and interests of those at different language levels.

Greetings and announcements should be in both languages. Bilingual publicity, media, signage, and welcome areas are essential, documentation and any documents should be bilingual and/or available in both languages, and translators/interpreters may be needed. While the principles are the same whether an event is face-to-face or virtual/online, but technology can help with subtitles and accompanying text in the other language available. However, it is important to maximize the use of bilingual organizers and participants rather than automated translation in the interest of community building and authentic communication.

The program content also needs to be bilingual in its philosophy. While every word does not have to be translated, it is important to have enough material in both languages so that everyone is comfortable, even those who are not completely bilingual. For example, a talk can be given in either language, and even if simultaneous interpretation may not be available, the presentation slides should be bilingual, or presented in both languages. Organizational websites and social media, along with publications, can and should be bilingual.

And this raises the question of how to create a bilingual community. Beyond a particular event or publication, it is important to consider how best to manage both languages on an ongoing basis in order to further develop language skills among those who have varying levels of skills, giving proficient and fluent community members the opportunities to practice their skills and to grow as speakers and language users while not excluding or stressing community members who have fewer or no language knowledge. The concept of high/low is one approach – high interest events with relatively low reliance on language in order to bring the community together. In addition, there needs to be a variety of opportunities for community members to learn and use the target language/*langue d'arrivee* in authentic settings and for authentic purposes and to have the opportunity to discuss the challenges of language learning and of making a conscious decision to become bilingual. Discussions of self-directed independent learning and of making language a habit in daily life are essential to long-term behavior change.

The role of the mother tongue or fluent speaker is also essential to examine. While the fluent speaker may seem likely to play a starring or leadership role in the movement, language learners – and even those who do not speak the language or have not yet become language learners – have an equally important role to play. The interest in language learning and the dynamic of developing language use and fluency play a central role in the advancement of French language and Francophone culture, and motivated learners and supporters of French language learning play a central role in developing opportunities to learn French and to use French to varying degrees, essential to rebuilding the use of French.

It is also important for community members to develop a sense of French/Francophone identity, along with a global mindset. While this may seem relatively simple and straightforward, it is important to remember that history is written by those in power militarily, politically, and economically, and that this history is written not only from their perspective but also – importantly – in their language. In order to develop this French/Francophone identity, it is important to have local and regional history concerning the French heritage experience written from a French/Francophone perspective and in French or in both languages. In the US, the narrative of US history has generally been framed by our British colonial experience, while in fact, the British colonial period was relatively short and extended only over an extremely small portion of what is now the US. A reenvisioning of US history and culture written from a Francophone perspective is sorely needed.

However, we all live in a globalized and interconnected world, and it is important to consider the role and significance of the French language and knowledge of the Francophone world in the development of an international mindset, global identity, and values of global citizenship. The French language has long been renowned as a language of ideas, including those which inspired the American Revolution. As a global language, French is used around the world and is the language of expression of a wide range of ideas. In addition, France is a world leader in global health, environmental issues, and many other areas.

A challenge facing French heritage and Francophone communities in the US is to maximize the impact of French and Francophone ideas and values in their own lives and in our society. In order to foster and encourage understanding and discussion of these ideas and values in our society, it is necessary for community members not only to explore these values in their personal lives but also to engage in these public conversations and social movements and to participate as thought leaders and influencers, bringing French and Francophone ideas and values, along with a demonstration of the overall value of the French language, to the attention of mainstream community and media.

Conclusions – The Future of French

The advancement of the French language and Francophone culture in the US is certainly based on the three pillars – learning, communication, and creativity – of the current French government campaign to promote French throughout the world, but it is also a social movement, which typically brings together many perspectives united by a shared purpose (Satell & Popovic, 2017). In this case, the development of a sustainable French language and Francophone community in the US is the shared purpose, and potential supporters of the social movement for French, French and Franco activists, include not only those who already speak French but also those who are interested in finding out more, and those who may not yet even realize that they may be interested. The social and political tactics and strategies used in social movements around the world and throughout history, as well as those currently used in the US, especially media, communication, and education.

For those who may question the need for community building, it is important to bear in mind the importance of a sense of community in terms of individual self-esteem, but also in terms of equity and social justice for the community, with language learning opportunity through immersion programs in public schools as just one example. Activists in a Francophone community building initiative will need to make choices, based on goals and capabilities, between in-person events and activities and a physical center, or virtual initiatives. Some issues in community building with special relevance for the building and rebuilding of Francophone communities are developing a sense of place, whether regional or global virtual or on-site, social interaction and the development of interpersonal ties, joint action in support of shared goals and purpose, etc. Community building has taken on a greater importance as a result of the COVID-19 pandemic, with an increased need to strengthen ties among us. It is also important to consider the nature of the ties between individuals and groups in this movement and community. While it is natural to consider that strong ties will be more effective and lasting, weak ties also play an important role in that strong ties will unite members of a particular group within a social movement or community, but weak ties have the ability to unite many, which is exactly what is needed for an effective and successful movement. In terms of language advocacy, these weak ties – the opportunity to use the language at random moments, in casual encounters, and in all types of low-stakes conversations – are invaluable in building the habit of language use. While technology has been cited as a factor in the erosion and decline of community ties (Putnam, 2000), technology can recreate to some extent the weak ties that are so important to a social movement.

Conclusions – The Future of French

Languages exist in formal settings like schools and the workplace, as well as within the home. However, in terms of social movements and of community building as a language advocacy activism, the importance of third places – coffee houses, libraries, and community spaces – as the heart of community interaction (Oldenburg, 1999), should be included in any initiative to rebuild the Francophone community. The numerous possibilities for the learning and use of French in these "third places" include, but are not limited to, language tables, book discussion groups, informal entertainment events, etc.

The Role of Leadership in French Language Advocacy

Leadership is essential to effective advocacy, community building, and social movements, and may be defined as "a process whereby an individual influences a group of individuals to achieve a common goal." Building French language skills and the Francophone community is definitely a process that includes both short-term objectives and long-term goals. It is an interactive, transactional event, as is language itself. Leadership also involves influence of an individual or small group on a larger number of people, in this case those who are currently or potentially interested in the French language and Francophone culture (Northouse, 2013). Leadership brings together diverse individuals and groups for a shared purpose, the pursuit of a common goal, and the resurgence of French language and Francophone culture. It is important to note that this concept of social and community leadership – a process, and transactional in nature – is not limited to those with a particular trait such as education or position, and is available to all.

A particular form of leadership is that of the social media influencer (SMI), who also has a pivotal role to play in the campaign for the resurgence of French. In terms of democratizing influence, anyone can be a social influencer. As social media is not necessarily tied to a traditional community, important factors to consider are how to build your audience and keep them engaged, how to package your message and appeal to potential stakeholders and allies, and how to engage in your advocacy in a positive manner. It is important to note that social media is accessible to most, and that many voices can bring a French language and Francophone culture to the public conversation.

In order to bring about the resurgence of French, the impact of political support is considerable, and it is also necessary to seek support from public figures and elected officials. An advocacy event in which French language supporters would personally make the case for French to their elected officials, either in person or virtually, is an important part of making French a community issue and in bringing French into the public conversation. Strategy for the French language activist is based on innovation, characterized by the importance of the window of opportunity.

In order to bring about the resurgence of French, a social movement is in order, grounded in community building, leadership, social media influence, and innovation, with a goal of bringing together many voices in support of the shared goal of building French language skills and the Francophone community.

The Role of French Language Skills and Fluency

While those who are fluent in the target language, in this case French, play an essential role as language users, models, and teachers, those who have limited or even no language skills can play a leadership role, with motivation and community ties as frequent advantages. The case of the significance of education is similar, with educators having long played the leadership role in advocating for and promoting language learning. Those who may not be educators and may not have advanced degrees can also play a crucial role, especially through their personal engagement as parents, heritage or mother tongue speakers, and community leaders. Business and government at all levels can offer support through internships, grants, etc. Leadership is a question that often arises in any community building or social movement, and it is important to realize that anyone can be a leader. Often individuals believe that a leader must be a person with certain political, professional, or educational qualifications, but the reality is that anyone can play a leadership role in a community or social movement, if they have the desire to do so. Building and rebuilding the Francophone community in the US is a grassroots movement with room for many voices, many skills, and many styles.

A significant issue in building French language skills and Francophone community in the US does, however, lies in language learning. There are, of course, multiple aspects involved – the age of the learner, the learning environment, the goals of the learners, etc. One point that is important to highlight is that language learning in the classroom, within an educational institution, is the purview of professional educators, their institutions, and external governing factors. This means that French language learning within our institutions is developed and implemented by professional educators in accordance with best practices for K-16 education.

What is of interest to the French language stakeholder or activist within the context of community building or a social movement is community-based learning and related language learning and language use activities and opportunities. As far as French learning beyond our educational institutions is concerned, the worldwide *Alliance Française* is the best-known example, although the Alliance is more highly structured than many grassroots efforts are likely to be.

While the idea of language learning unrelated to schools and colleges may seem unusual, it has actually had a place in the US for many years, often under the auspices of a sociocultural organization or religious institution. This more informal type of language instruction and learning has advantages and disadvantages. Among the advantages would be flexibility in terms of settings, teachers, and methodologies, along with the ability to draw on community resources in terms of authentic learning and preprofessional and internship opportunities, as well as for motivational support and funding. Flexibility also extends to the inclusion of learners who might not otherwise have access to language learning, either because French may not be available through the local public schools or because they may not be able to attend a traditional college class for any number of reasons, including cost, travel, family and work commitments, etc. However, the most important advantage of community-based language learning is its ability to highlight and in some instances to highlight, and in some cases to revive, local language aspects along with the more standardized and international language elements. While this informal model could favor individualized instruction and growth in both language skills and cultural knowledge and the resulting increase in self-esteem, there is no widely recognized credential or badge unless the language learning initiative within the broader community building and social movement develops a partnership with an established curriculum or program.

An examination of curriculum within educational institutions, especially at the postsecondary level where enrollments have declined, may also reveal potential new directions. Motivation and immersion have long been considered the most effective predictors of language learning outcome, and in a situation where language learning is a choice, or an elective course, in many cases, creating and strengthening motivation through a variety of approaches is key, and immersion is to be considered. Although public school immersion programs are ideal in that they offer to all the opportunity for language learning and intercultural understanding, summer language camps for all ages, short-term immersion experiences, and presemester language boot camps for college and university students are just a few of the many possibilities. In all cases, flexibility and an understanding of the language learner are key to success.

Conclusions – The Future of French

The use of French in the US is perhaps an even more complex topic that the learning of French. While teaching and learning are tangible concepts that we are generally familiar with, along with their settings and support materials, the creation of sustainable opportunities to use French in the US is a relatively unfamiliar concept. On the level of the individual speaker and local community, it is a question of maintaining and strengthening language skills and expanding opportunities for language use among those who are already proficient, fluent, or mother tongue speakers. However, the numbers of Americans of French heritage far surpass the number of those who currently speak French in the home, the importance of expanding the use of French among them is clear. The challenge remains how to do this, and how to appeal to those among whom their French heritage is partially lost or forgotten in the mists of time. One way to do this would be for them to learn French, but before they even take that first step, the idea must have sufficient appeal to drive continued learning. Although each individual has different interests, one way to enhance the appeal of learning French is to provide interesting opportunities for its use in everyday life here in the US. Career opportunities including internships in French-speaking countries or in French companies in the US are a starting point, and scholarships and achievement awards for students of French would be another. However, life extends beyond the classroom and the workplace, so the popular culture is the primary area of interest.

Of course, building the Francophone community has two sides – advocating for the learning and use of the French language and for the understanding of French and Francophone culture in the mainstream culture and among the French heritage and Francophone community; and advocating for the newest arrivals among US Francophones by working to ensure that the children of Francophone immigrant families have the opportunity to maintain their family language. This two-pronged initiative involves working to help those who may not yet be familiar with our institutions and our language to become effective advocates for their own children and communities.

French is considered one of only two global languages, widely used around the world, because of the culture and history of France, and of the *attractivité* of France and of French culture, lifestyle, ideas, and values. Well over 200M speak French worldwide, and the number of French speakers is predicted to dramatically increase, possibly making French the most widely spoken language in the world in the coming decades, largely due to the dynamic demographic growth of Africa, home to the majority of French speakers worldwide and where the language is growing rapidly in importance, viewed by many. With nearly 90 members, the *Organisation internationale de la Francophonie* (OIF), observing its 50th anniversary in 2020, is a unique and powerful reflection of the worldwide role of France, of French ideas and values, and of Francophone culture. Not only do its cultural arts enjoy worldwide renown and have done so for centuries, but French is also considered one of the most valuable languages in international business, and more international visitors make Paris their destination each year than any other city in the world (English, Chinese, French, 2011). In addition, French is the second most widely studied language in the world, and Francophiles – those who love all things French – are found in large numbers everywhere, a unique phenomenon in a world where often language learning and use are driven by more tangible motivations.

The soft power – influence of French language, culture, lifestyle, ideas, and values – in the world is undisputable everywhere but in the US, where French language learning has declined so dramatically that programs in colleges and universities across the country are in danger of dramatic cutbacks and closure, with the French language the most severely impacted in recent years.

The future of French is bright worldwide, with the presence of France, along with its language and culture, growing worldwide, and the Francophone world growing in political, economic, social, and global importance. However, in the US, while French remains the second most popular foreign language studied, French programs in colleges and universities are increasingly at risk, and French language learning is part of a broader picture in US education that includes a crisis of the humanities, a birth dearth predicted to dramatically impact higher education enrollment, budget challenges exacerbated by the COVID-19 pandemic, and the decrease in oil prices. At the elementary and middle school levels, French learning is impacted by the lack of opportunity for students to begin language learning at an early age, highlighted by the small and decreasing number of foreign languages. The relatively small number of language learners, including those enrolled in French, results in an insufficient number of college and university students with the sufficient motivation and skills to support sustainable preprofessional programs in French. Even the growing number of French immersion programs, a bright spot in an otherwise bleak scenario, is insufficient to reverse the overall trend.

Despite this challenging environment, there are some encouraging signs. In a recent survey, a significant number of Americans responded that they wished they had learned another language while in school, and foreign language educators, including French language educators, aware of the need for advocacy, have been engaged in supporting and defending at-risk programs and in making known the benefits of language learning and, specifically, of French language learning. Our neighbors to the north, in Canada and in Québec, have moved into the second 50 years of official French and English bilingualism and offer a model and road map for the US in many areas. Perhaps most importantly, significant numbers of Francophones, including not only French nationals but also many from around the Francophone, have been making their home in the US in recent years and increasing the number of those who actively use French in their daily lives and who speak French in the home, important factors in maintaining language vitality and keeping French alive in the US.

Within a generally challenging US context for French, there is tremendous effort needed in order to bring about a resurgence of French in alignment with the current and predicted significance of French globally. Both short-term and long-term initiatives need to be developed and implemented, as does advocacy both within educational institutions and within the broader society.

We all need to advocate for opportunity for all interested students to have access to continued foreign language learning – including French – from the earliest grade levels. Among educators, there is already a growing realization that advocacy is an ongoing need everywhere, involving everyone, and that advocacy efforts need to range from online and in-person events to curriculum reform. French language advocacy also needs to include the well over 10M Americans of French ancestry, who have the potential not only as heritage language speakers but also as supporters of Francophone initiatives and events.

In addition to the partnerships among French language educators at all levels and among foreign language educators, partnerships are needed with the Francophone community and French heritage groups, as well as with supporters of French language and culture often referred to as Francophiles, with an eye to external partners including the French government with its extensive linguistic and cultural resources and expertise, as well as the current campaign in support of French.

However, the challenge remains to encourage more students in the US to learn French and more US communities and organizations to encourage its use, and to encourage and support its use in the media, the arts, and public life. Paradoxically, while French is one of the three top languages both for international business and in terms of demand in the US workplace, there are relatively few career pathways available to high school and college students interested in working in French (ACTFL, 2019; English, Chinese, French, 2011). In addition, while French is one of the two global languages and global citizenship is of interest to many young people, relatively few pathways to students interested in volunteer and professional roles in support of global citizenship.

Despite its role as a global language and as a language in the US since the earliest years of European exploration, French remains surprising invisible relative both to English and to other languages present in the US, and this invisibility extends to French culture and the arts, and even to those who speak French, among many in the US. Increasing awareness in the US in terms of the presence of French around the world and here at home could go a long way toward increasing interest in learning more about the people, the culture, and the language.

Promotion of French Worldwide

In 2018, the then newly elected President of France Emmanuel Macron announced a campaign to promote the French language worldwide, especially in Africa (Chutel, 2018; France Diplomacy, Africa and Francophonie, 2019; O'Mahony, 2019), the area of largest growth in the number of French speakers. French institutions supporting the French language worldwide include the Institut Français, the Francophonie, TV5Monde, and Radio France Internationale. This closely followed the announcement of a new fund to support French–English bilingual programs in the US, made by Macron during his September visit to New York to address the United Nations General Assembly, and which includes support for teacher training and student exchange programs.

This international strategy for the French language and multilingualism "is based on 33 measures to learn, communicate and create in French." This initiative includes both a bilateral policy stressing cooperation with local authorities in other countries and a multilateral policy stressing unity within the Francophone nations and support of the OIF.

Re-inventing French language Learning and Advocacy

The fact remains that, despite the usefulness of French in the workplace and in our personal lives, French language learning has declined in the US in recent years. While it remains the second most popular additional language studied at all levels, programs have been cut or eliminated especially at the college and university level. However, it is necessary to bear in mind that French exists within a variety of contexts in the US, as it does throughout the world. It exists in a North American context where it is one of many languages spoken, it exists within the educational, social, and budgetary context of a specific institution or school district. It exists within a curricular context where it may compete with other disciplines and even with other languages for enrollment, staffing, and funding. It also exists, especially at the college and university level, within the context of the crisis of the humanities, and any decrease in the number of students majoring in French or in the number of undergraduate and graduate programs inevitably impacts the number of qualified teachers available to replace positions in any new or expanded program, as well as vacancies and positions available due to retirement.

If a resurgence of French in the US is to occur, it will be necessary to reimagine, to rethink, and to reinvent French language learning and advocacy in the US – before it is too late. While the recent growth of French immersion programs in US public schools often referred to as the Bilingual Revolution and the membership of the US state of Louisiana in the OIF are high-profile examples of alternative pathways for French language learning and use in the US, these programs need to be available to more students through replication and adaptation to local needs. At the present time, many US students do not have access to continued French language learning, and despite the need for French language skills among US employers, relatively few career pathways exist for students proficient in French.

For all these reasons, it is necessary to reenvision the role and presence of French in the US and to rethink French language learning and the use of French in the workplace and in our communities. As a first step it is necessary to reexamine French language and Francophone culture within the whole of society. In light of the importance of French both as a global language and as a US language in terms of our cultural identity and history, it is necessary to engage in backward design in order to develop the learning, cultural, social, and preprofessional pathways and experiences needed for French to flourish and thrive in the North American space.

Envisioning a society where French is used in our homes and communities, where French is a language of culture, creativity, media, and socialization, and where French is routinely used in a globalized workplace in a multilingual US, it is necessary to create social, business, and cultural opportunities in partnership with local

Francophone groups and with Francophone organizations worldwide. This would logically entail reciprocal investment of effort and resources in the creation of business, cultural, and educational exchanges and opportunities. As a result of these opportunities, demand for French language skills would be highlighted and even more obvious to governmental and educational decision-makers, leading to increased opportunity for continued learning of French and to a curriculum including preprofessional language skills across the disciplines. A multidisciplinary and pragmatic approach would also lead to an increased emphasis on experiential learning and internships in French and Francophone organizations. However, as important as the workplace and career considerations undeniably are, the whole of society must be considered, and this means not only an opportunity for students to learn French and to have access to internships and other experiential learning opportunities, it also implies access to learning for all ages as well as access to creative and media opportunities for which France and the *Francophonie* have long been well known. A reenvisioned presence of French language and Francophone culture would also include the actualization of the whole person and the valorization of individual and personal creativity in the arts and reflected in a robust media presence.

The challenge – and goal – of this new vision would be a revitalization of French language and Francophone culture in the public conversation, with Francophones and French language learners of all ages encouraged, but with an emphasis on developing a new generation of Francophones able to develop both a French and Francophone identity and a global mindset at the same time.

Action steps include a proactive French language advocacy campaign, characterized by a broad support for foreign language learning and use generally, and for French language learning and use specifically, with language stakeholders supporting both established campaigns at all levels. In addition, as language is a unique communicative tool in building relationships, the use of French whenever possible is essential, especially in Francophone, Francophile, and Franco-American homes and communities. Discussion groups, clubs, and other activities, groups, and events where French is spoken need to be prioritized. Online and social media, along with books, blogs, newsletters, and broadcast media like radio and television stations are all part of building the French language presence. Equally important are opportunities for all interested students to learn French and for those proficient in French to access preprofessional and professional experiences and opportunities. The master's program in Professional

French at the University of Wisconsin and the initiative launched by the Paris Chamber of Commerce to train faculty in the teaching of professional French, are wonderful example, as are the *Oui!* Initiative and the French language job fair in Louisiana. It is important to note that a similar approach would be valid for many other languages in the US.

Concluding Thoughts

Coming full circle, it is important to remember that French is a global language on the rise, powered by not only the "soft power" or influence of France but also – and perhaps more importantly – its dynamic growth as a language of culture, communication, education, information, and business, around the world, especially in Africa. In the US, however, French remains remarkably low-profile, with Francophones relatively invisible in the media, popular culture, and public conversation. With over 10M Americans of French heritage, and with over 2M in the US speaking French at home, this is paradoxical, even more so given the role of French in the Americas and throughout the world.

In a globalized and interconnected world, the relationship and exchange of ideas between the Americans and the French, our closest friends and oldest allies will inevitably lead to closer ties, supported by our shared history and values and by our current and future generations of bilingual global citizens. This understanding and appreciation of French and Francophone culture, supported by French language learning and – most importantly – *use* of French in our homes and communities, in the workplace, and in our society, will encourage not only a better understanding of our own American cultural identity but also increased tolerance. Knowledge of the French language and an understanding of Francophone culture will empower Americans not only to better appreciate the humanistic values of France and of the Francophonie but also to engage more effectively as global citizens in the global conversation.

While the future is trending positive for the French language in the world and in the US, the future is by no means assured. Languages are constantly in contact, and their influence and perceived value evolve due to a variety of factors both globally and locally. French is no exception – while the power of French ideas and values along with the contribution of France to our civilization and history are clear,

DOI: 10.4324/9781003023760-11

globalization and the interconnectedness of the globalized world – made even more evident by the COVID-19 pandemic – have created a new world, a new normal, and some would even say a new world order/*ont changé la donne*. There is a sense of urgency, and the time to act is now.

The French government has led the way in its campaign for French, grounded in and framed by learning, communication, and creativity, and in its launch of the new online *Dictionnaire des Francophones* in 2021. It is time for French language stakeholders everywhere to engage in advocacy for the learning and use of French, to be willing to commit to leadership roles as needed, and to turn their French language resolutions into habits – making the learning and use of French part of their daily lives.

The time of *survivance* is past, and our present and future call for *francoresponsabilité* in order to build a sustainable Francophone future or *francodurabilité* – so that French will not just survive, but thrive.

French has been a part of our past and is clearly a part of our present, but the future is up to us – Francophones, Franco-Americans, and Francophiles – as individuals, in our communities, and as global citizens (OIF, 2021). *L'union fait la force!*

References

Adams, M., & Carfagna, A. (2006). *Coming of Age in a Globalized World: The Next Generation*. Westport, CT: Kumarian.
Agence pour l'enseignement français à l'étranger. (2021). https://www.aefe.fr
Agence universitaire de la Francophonie. (n.d.). https://www.auf.org/
American Academy of Arts and Sciences (AMACAD). (2017). America's Languages: Investing in Language Education for the 21st Century. https://www.amacad.org/publication/americas-languages
American Academy of Arts and Sciences (AMACAD). (2020). The Importance of Languages in Global Context: A Call to Action. https://www.amacad.org/news/global-languages-importance
American Council on the Teaching of Foreign Languages (ACTFL). (2017). Educators Rising 2.0. https://www.actfl.org/advocacy/educators-rising
American Council on the Teaching of Foreign Languages (ACTFL). Lead with Languages. (2019). Making Languages Our Business: Addressing Foreign Language Demand among U.S. Employers. https://www.leadwithlanguages.org/language-advocacy/publications/
American Association of Teachers of French (AATF). (2019). www.frenchteachers.org
Alliance Francaise. Alliances Francaises Canada. http://www.af.ca/about-af/
Alliance Française. https://afusa.org/about-the-alliance-francaise/
Associated Press. (2021). Louisiana, France Renew Educational, Professional Agreement. https://www.klfy.com/louisiana/louisiana-france-renew-educational-professional-agreement/
Association of the French Schools in North America (AFSA). Association of the French Schools in North America. http://www.aefa-afsa.org/
Barr, L. (2014). *Provence, 1970: M.F.K. Fisher, Julia Child, James Beard, and the Reinvention of American Taste*. New York: Clarkson Potter.
BBC. (n.d.). Languages across Europe: Monaco. (Accessed November 3, 2021).
BBC News. (2017.) Brexit: English Language 'Losing Importance' – EU's Juncker. https://www.bbc.com/news/world-europe-39816044
Belluck, P. (2006). Long-Scorned in Maine, French Has Renaissance. https://www.nytimes.com/2006/06/04/us/04french.html

Blatt, B. (2014). Tagalog in California, Cherokee in Arkansas: What Language Does Your State Speak? https://slate.com/culture/2014/05/language-map-whats-the-most-popular-language-in-your-state.html

Bordman, A. (2018). *Everyday Monet: A Giverny-Inspired Gardening and Lifestyle Guide to Living Your Best Impressionist Life.* New York: Dey Street.

Bourdillon, Y. (2019). Why French Will Remain the "Other" Global Language. https://worldcrunch.com/culture-society/why-french-will-remain-the-other-global-language

Boutroy, G. (2021). C'est terminé pour le Réseau des villes francophones et francophiles d'Amérique. https://ici.radio-canada.ca/nouvelle/1764105/fin-reseau-villes-francophones-francophiles-amerique-centre-francophonie

British Council. (2013). The English Effect. https://www.britishcouncil.org/sites/default/files/english-effect-report-v2.pdf

Bulgur, A. (2021). Spiritual Food: How French Books Feed the Soul. https://france-amerique.com/en/spiritual-food-how-french-books-feed-the-soul/

Business France. (n.d.). Ambition Africa. https://www.businessfrance.fr/ambition-africa-2021

Business France. (n.d.). Who Are We? https://www.businessfrance.fr/en/about-us

Business France. (2018). France's Global Economy. https://www.businessfrance.fr/discover-france-in-depth-france-s-global-economy

Campus France. Choose France Summit. (2021). https://www.campusfrance.org/en/choose-france-summit

Canone, M. (2019). French-Language Business Initiative Designed to Help International Visitors to La. (Louisiana) https://katc.com/news/covering-louisiana/2019/03/28/french-language-business-initiative-designed-to-help-international-visitors-to-la/

Carmosino, E. (2021). 80 International Teachers Hired to Teach French and Spanish Immersion Programs in Louisiana. https://www.theadvocate.com/baton_rouge/news/education/article_9addd af2-ebe0-11eb-89e6-57809f732a7b.html

Carrere, C. (2014). Francophonie Would Provide Significant Stability in Times of Crisis. https://ferdi.fr/en/publications/francophonie-would-provide-significant-stability-in-times-of-crisis

CCI France International. (2021). Nos Missions. https://www.ccifrance-international.org/qui-sommes-nous/nos-missions.html

CCI France Japon. (CCIFJ). (2021). The French Chamber of Commerce in Japan. https://www.ccifj.or.jp/en/the-chamber.html

CCI France Japon. (2021). French Companies Fair: Knowing French Companies 2020. https://www.ccifj.or.jp/emploi-et-formation/french-companies-fair.html

CCI France Vietnam. (CCIFV). (2021). CCI France-Vietnam. https://www.ccifv.org/en.html

Center for Strategic and International Studies (CSIS). (2018). Mapping the U.S.-Canada Energy Relationship. https://www.csis.org/analysis/mapping-us-canada-energy-relationship

References

Chambre de Commerce France-Canada (CCFC). (2021). Chambre de Commerce France-Canada. https://www.ccfc-france-canada.com/

Chambre de Commerce Franco-Arabe (CCFA). (2021). https://ccfranco-arabe.fr/

Chambre de Commerce France-Canada. (2021). Missions de la Chambre de Commerce France-Canada. https://www.ccfc-france-canada.com/nous-connaitre/notre-histoire-nos-mission

Chan, K. (2016). These Are the Most Powerful Languages in the World. https://www.weforum.org/agenda/2016/12/these-are-the-most-powerful-languages-in-the-world/

Chrisafis, A. (2018). Macron Launches Drive to Boost French Language around World. https://www.theguardian.com/world/2018/mar/20/macron-launches-drive-to-boost-french-language-around-world

Chrisafis, A. (2019). Beyoncé and Jay-Z help Louvre Museum Break Visitor Record in 2018. https://www.theguardian.com/world/2019/jan/03/beyonce-jay-z-help-louvre-museum-break-visitor-record

Chutel, L. (2018). French Is Now the Fifth Most Spoken World Language and Growing – Thanks to Africans. https://www.weforum.org/agenda/2018/10/french-is-now-the-fifth-most-spoken-world-language-and-growing-thanks-to-africans/

Conseil pour le Developpement du Francais en Louisiane. (CODOFIL). (2021) Agence Des Affaires Francophones. Oui! FrancoResponsable. L'Initiative Oui! *The Oui! Initiative* https://www.crt.state.la.us/cultural-development/codofil/programs/francoresponsable/

Cooke, K. (2021). BrandZ Top 50 Most Valuable French Brands 2019. https://www.kantar.com/inspiration/brands/brandz-top-50-most-valuable-french-brands-2019

Cultural Services. French Embassy United States. (2021a). French Books in the US – The Updated 2020 Edition. https://frenchculture.org/books-and-ideas/12239-french-books-us-2020-edition

Cultural Services. French Embassy in the United States. (2019). French Heritage Language Programs. https://frenchlanguagek12.org/french-heritage

Cultural Services. French Embassy United States. (2019). French Language Job Fair in New Orleans. https://frenchhighereducation.org/job-fairs/new-orleans

Cultural Services. French Embassy United States. (2021b). Job Fairs. https://frenchhighereducation.org/job-fairs

Daly, J.A. (2011). *Advocacy: Championing Ideas and Influencing Others*. New Haven, CT: Yale.

Daniellson, K.S. (2017). The Benefits of Speaking More Than One Language. https://www.weforum.org/agenda/2017/04/the-benefits-of-speaking-more-than-one-language/

De Jean, J. (2005). *The Essence of Style: How the French Invented High Fashion, Fine Food, Chic Cafes, Style, Sophistication, and Glamour.* New York: Free Press.

References

Dieudonne, E. (2017). Montreal: Gateway City for French Companies in North America. https://www.indexwebmarketing.com/en/montreal-gateway-city-for-french-companies-in-north-america/

Economic Relations between Canada and France. https://www.canadainternational.gc.ca/france/bilateral_relations_bilaterales/canada_france_comm_brief_resume.aspx?lang=eng#:~:text=These%20include%20Aastra%2C%20Bombardier%2C%20the,a%20major%20investor%20in%20Canada.

Egginton, (2019). Is Computer Code a Foreign Language? https://www.nytimes.com/2019/03/17/opinion/code-foreign-language.html

English, Chinese, French Most Useful for Business. (2011). https://www.languagemagazine.com/english-chinese-french-most-useful-for-business/

European Commission (EC). (2012). Eurobarometer. Europeans and Their Languages. https://ec.europa.eu/commfrontoffice/publicopinion/archives/ebs/ebs_386_en.pdf

European Union. France. (2021). (https://europa.eu/european-union/about-eu/countries/member-countries/france_en

FACE Foundation. (2021). The French Language Heritage Program. https://face-foundation.org/language-education/french-heritage-language-program/

Fausset, R. (2015). In Louisiana, Desire for a French Renaissance https://www.nytimes.com/2015/02/15/us/in-louisiana-desire-for-a-french-renaissance.html

Fausset, R. (2019). Louisiana says 'Oui' to French, Amid Explosion in Dual-Language Schools. https://www.nytimes.com/2019/08/21/us/louisiana-french-dual-language.html

Federal Council. (2020). Multilingualism. https://www.eda.admin.ch/aboutswitzerland/en/home/gesellschaft/sprachen/mehrsprachigkeit.html

Fillak, J. (2018). In Maine, French Culture Experiences a Revival. https://frenchly.us/the-decline-of-francophone-communities-in-maine/

Fischer, D.H. (2008). *Champlain's Dream*. New York: Simon & Schuster.

FocusEconomics. (2020). France Economic Outlook. https://www.focus-economics.com/countries/france

Fondation des Alliances Françaises. (2017). Les Alliances Francaises dans le Monde, 2017. https://www.fondation-alliancefr.org/wp-content/uploads/AF_Rapport_Data_2017.pdf

Fortune Global 500. (2020). France. https://fortune.com/global500/2019/search/?hqcountry=France

France 24. (2021). New French Dictionary Aims to Embrace Diversity of World's Francophones. https://www.france24.com/en/europe/20210316-new-french-dictionary-aims-to-embrace-diversity-of-world-s-francophones

France Country Commercial Guide. (2019). France: Market Overview. https://www.export.gov/article?series=a0pt0000000PAtnAAG&type=Country_Commercial__kav

France Diplomacy. (2019). Africa and Francophonie. https://www.diplomatie.gouv.fr/en/country-files/africa/africa-and-francophonie/

France Diplomacy. (2019). Economic Relations between France and Africa. https://www.diplomatie.gouv.fr/en/country-files/africa/economic-relations-between-france-and-africa/
France Diplomacy. (2019). Entrepreneurship and Investing in France. https://www.diplomatie.gouv.fr/en/french-foreign-policy/economic-diplomacy-foreign-trade/entrepreneurship-and-investing-in-france/
France Diplomacy. (2019). France and the United States. https://www.diplomatie.gouv.fr/en/country-files/united-states/france-and-united-states/
France Diplomacy. (2019). Institutions Promoting the French Language. https://www.diplomatie.gouv.fr/en/french-foreign-policy/francophony-and-the-french-language/institutions-promoting-the-french-language/
France Diplomacy. (2019). The French School System Abroad (AEFE). https://www.diplomatie.gouv.fr/en/french-foreign-policy/francophony-and-the-french-language/learning-and-teaching-french/the-french-school-system-abroad-aefe/
France Diplomacy (2021). France and Brazil. https://www.diplomatie.gouv.fr/en/country-files/brazil/
France Diplomacy. (2021). French diplomacy in Africa: Global issues. https://www.diplomatie.gouv.fr/en/country-files/africa/french-diplomacy-in-africa-global-issues/ (2017). https://www.diplomatie.gouv.fr/IMG/pdf/1374-infographie_relations_france_argentine_versionaccessible_cle4b8fcc.pdf
France Diplomacy. (2021). Francophony and the French Language. https://www.diplomatie.gouv.fr/en/french-foreign-policy/francophony-and-the-french-language/
France Diplomacy. (2021) International Strategy for the French Language and Multilingualism. https://www.diplomatie.gouv.fr/en/french-foreign-policy/francophony-and-the-french-language/international-strategy-for-the-french-language-and-multilingualism/
France Diplomacy. (2021). Tourism. https://www.diplomatie.gouv.fr/en/french-foreign-policy/tourism/
Franceinfo. (2021). Cité internationale de la langue française: Emmanuel Macron espère inaugurer le château rénové de Villers-Cotterêts en mars 2022. https://www.francetvinfo.fr/culture/patrimoine/cite-internationale-de-la-langue-francaise-macron-espere-inaugurer-le-chateau-renove-de-villers-cotterets-en-mars-2022_4339677.html
Franco-Arab Chamber of Commerce. (2020). France & the Middle East. https://middleeast-business.com/france-the-middle-east/
French-American Chamber of Commerce. https://nationalfacc.org/
French Diplomacy. (2010). French External Action for Education in Developing Countries: 2010–2015. https://www.diplomatie.gouv.fr/IMG/pdf/Education_in_developing_countries_en.pdf
(2021). French Morning Staff. (2017). The French Population Has Officially Increased in North America. https://frenchly.us/french-population-officially-increased-north-america/
French Treasury in the US. (2017). The French Economic Footprint in the US. https://frenchtreasuryintheus.org/en/the-french-economic-footprint-in-the-u-s/

French Treasury in the US. (2019). *The United States & France: 2019 Economic Report.* https://frenchtreasuryintheus.org/wp-content/uploads/2019/09/2019-France-U.S.-economic_full-report.pdf

Fumaroli, M. (2011). *When the World Spoke French.* New York: New York Review Books Classics

Gagliano, K. (2019). Lafayette Area Businesses Encouraged to Just Say 'oui' to Keeping French Language Alive. https://www.theadvocate.com/acadiana/news/article_b96e8628-4db4-11e9-b987-8f521cb8f779.html

Galvin, G. (2016). Some Say Computer Coding Is a Foreign Language. https://www.usnews.com/news/stem-solutions/articles/2016-10-13/spanish-french-python-some-say-computer-coding-is-a-foreign-language

Gaudry, F. (2018). *Let's Eat France.* New York: Artisan.

Gobry, P-E. (2014). Want to Know the Language of the Future? The Data Suggests It Might Be... French. https://www.forbes.com/sites/pascalemmanuelgobry/2014/03/21/want-to-know-the-language-of-the-future-the-data-suggests-it-could-be-french/#4d52d7f26d58

Godement, F. (2014). France's "Pivot" to Asia. https://ecfr.eu/wp-content/uploads/ECFR101_FRANCE_ASIA_BRIEF_AW_1.pdf

Gordon, P., & Meunier, S. (2001). *The French Challenge: Adopting to Globalization.* Washington, DC: Brookings.

Gordon, P., & Meunier, S. (2002). The French Economy's Adaptation to Globalization Has Been Remarkable. https://www.brookings.edu/on-the-record/the-french-economys-adaptation-to-globalization-has-been-remarkable/

Gouvernement du Grand-Duche du Luxembourg. (n.d.). Luxembourg: Let's Make It Happen. (Accessed November 8, 2021). https://luxembourg.public.lu/en/society-and-culture/languages/languages-spoken-luxembourg.html

Government of France. (2018). Choose France, The National Strategy to Attract More International Students. https://www.campusfrance.org/en/choose-france-strategie-attractivite-etudiants-internationaux-bienvenue-en-france

Government of France. (2019). Choose France: A Summit for Showcasing France's Economic Appeal. https://www.gouvernement.fr/en/choose-france-a-summit-for-showcasing-france-s-economic-appeal

Gray, A. (2017). France becomes the World No 1 for Soft Power. https://www.weforum.org/agenda/2017/07/france-new-world-leader-in-soft-power/

Grosjean, F. (2019). *A Journey in Languages and Cultures: The Life of a Bicultural Bilingual.* Oxford: Oxford University Press.

Grosjean, F. (2010; 2020). *Bilingualism's Best Kept Secret: More Than Half of the World's Population Is Bilingual.* https://www.psychologytoday.com/us/blog/life-bilingual/201011/bilingualisms-best-kept-secret

Guthridge, L. (2017). Don't Make Resolutions: Build Habits Instead. https://www.forbes.com/sites/forbescoachescouncil/2017/12/19/dont-make-resolutions-build-habits-instead/?sh=1c038b7757e5

Hardach, S. (2018). Speaking More Than One Language Can Boost Economic Booth. https://www.weforum.org/agenda/2018/02/speaking-more-languages-boost-economic-growth/

References

Hazan, J. (2016). Montreal Is Now Ranked the #4 Largest French Speaking City in The World. https://www.mtlblog.com/en-ca/news/montreal-is-now-ranked-}the-4-largest-french-speaking-city-in-the-world

Heath, R. (2017). Jean-Claude Juncker: 'English Is Losing Importance.' https://www.politico.eu/article/jean-claude-juncker-english-is-losing-importance/

Hogan-Brun, G. (2017). *Linguanomics: What is the Market Potential of Multilingualism?* New York: Bloomsbury.

Hu, (2018). Speaking a Second Language May Give Low-Income Kids a Boost. https://www.scientificamerican.com/article/speaking-a-second-language-may-give-low-income-kids-a-boost/

Institut Francais.(2021). La Culture francaise dans le monde. https://www.institutfrancais.com/fr

Institute for International Education (IIE). (2020). Fast Facts 2020. https://opendoorsdata.org/fast_facts/fast-facts-2020/

Ives, C. (2018). *Public Parks, Private Gardens: Paris to Provence.* New York: Metropolitan Museum of Art.

Jaumont, F. (2017). *The Bilingual Revolution: The Future of Education is in Two Languages.* New York: TBR Books.

Kanter, J., & Wolgelenter, M. (2017). EU Leader Says (in English) that English is Waning. https://www.nytimes.com/2017/05/05/world/europe/jean-claude-juncker-eu-english.html

Kharkhurin, A. (2012). *Multilingualism and Creativity.* Bristol: Multilingual Matters.

Kisluk-Grosheide, D., & Rondot, B., eds. (2018). *Visitors to Versailles: From Louis XIV to the French Revolution.* New York: Metropolitan Museum of Art.

Kotter, J. (2008). *A Sense of Urgency.* Boston, MA: Harvard Business Press.

L'AmCham France. (2021). Qui sommes-nous? http://amchamfrance.org/about-us/

http://www.bbc.co.uk/languages/european_languages/countries/monaco.shtml

Lee, N.R., & Kotler, P. (2015). *Social Marketing: Changing Behaviors for Good.* Thousand Oaks, CA: SAGE.

Livermore, D. (2016). *Driven by Difference: How Great Companies Fuel Innovation through Diversity.* New York: AMACOM.

Language Magazine. (2018). Louisiana Joins the Francophonie. https://www.languagemagazine.com/2018/10/12/louisiana-joins-la-francophonie/

Marshall, J. (2011). Africa: Francophone Teacher Training Spreads. https://www.universityworldnews.com/post.php?story=20110715180714963

Mazatlan Post. (2020). CCI France Japon. French Companies Fair: Knowing French Companies 2020. https://www.ccifj.or.jp/emploi-et-formation/french-companies-fair.html

Mazatlan Post. (2020). French Companies Are Targeting Mexico to Do Business with. https://themazatlanpost.com/2020/09/24/french-companies-are-targeting-mexico-to-do-business-with/

McCullough, D. (2011). *The Greater Journey: Americans in Paris*. New York: Simon & Schuster.

McFadden, C. (2020). 45+ of the Greatest French Inventions of All Time. https://interestingengineering.com/45-of-the-greatest-french-inventions-of-all-time

McGuire, P. (2016). African Immigrants Drive French-Speaking Renaissance in Maine. https://www.pressherald.com/2016/07/31/when-cultures-click-it-could-mean-a-renaissance-for-french-speaking-in-maine/

Meghelli, S. (2013). Hip-Hop à la Française. https://www.nytimes.com/roomfordebate/2013/10/14/is-france-becoming-too-american/hip-hop-a-la-francaise-29

Meltzer, M. (2020). They Love Paris in the Quarantine. https://www.nytimes.com/2020/11/05/style/french-expats.html

Modern Language Association (MLA). (2015). Data on Second Majors in Language and Literature: 2001–2013. https://www.mla.org/Resources/Research/Surveys-Reports-and-Other-Documents/Teaching-Enrollments-and-Programs/Data-on-Second-Majors-in-Language-and-Literature-2001-13

Modern Language Association (MLA). (2019). Enrollments in Languages Other Than English in United States Institutions of Higher Education. https://www.mla.org/Resources/Research/Surveys-Reports-and-Other-Documents/Teaching-Enrollments-and-Programs/Enrollments-in-Languages-Other-Than-English-in-United-States-Institutions-of-Higher-Education

Modern Language Association (MLA). (2007). Foreign Languages and Higher Education: New Structures for a Changed World. https://www.mla.org/Resources/Research/Surveys-Reports-and-Other-Documents/Teaching-Enrollments-and-Programs/Foreign-Languages-and-Higher-Education-New-Structures-for-a-Changed-World

Montlaur, B de. (2019). Do You Speak My Language? You Should. https://www.nytimes.com/2019/03/26/opinion/learn-foreign-language.html

Nadeau, J.-B. (2021). 33 Millions de Francophones dans les Amériques. https://www.ledevoir.com/societe/597077/de-la-terre-de-feu-a-la-terre-de-rupert-33-millions-de-francophones

New American Economy. (2017). Not Lost in Translation: U.S. Jobs Market Needs Foreign Language Skills. https://research.newamericaneconomy.org/report/not-lost-in-translation-the-growing-importance-of-foreign-language-skills-in-the-u-s-job-market/

Noreau, J. (2017). Trade between Quebec and the United States. https://www.desjardins.com/ressources/pdf/per0117e.pdf?resVer=1485876886000

Northouse, P.G. (2013). *Leadership: Theory and Practice*. 6th ed. Thousand Oaks, CA: SAGE.

Oldenburg, R. (1999). *The Great Good Place: Cafes, Coffee Shops, Bookstores, Bars, Hair Salons, and Other Hangouts at the Heart of a Community*. New York: Marlowe.

O'Mahony, J. (2019). Why the Future of French is African. https://www.bbc.com/news/world-africa-47790128

Organisation internationale de la Francophonie (OIF). (2014). La langue française dans le monde 2014 en image. https://www.youtube.com/watch?v=LqDClK_Za3M&t=70s

Organisation internationale de la Francophonie (OIF). (2018). La langue française dans le monde 2018 en image. https://www.youtube.com/watch?v=46HFrpkKJ-g&t=163sOrganisation internationale de la Francophonie (OIF). (2020). Rapport Consultation Jeunesse: La Francophonie de l'Avenir. https://redaction.consultation-jeunesse-francophonie.org/

Palet, L.S. (2014). Is French the language of the future? https://www.usatoday.com/story/news/world/2014/05/31/ozy-french-language/9781569/

Peckham, R.D. (n.d.). How French Is Ranked. https://www.utm.edu/staff/bobp/french/frank.shtml

Pratte, A., & Kay, J., eds. (2016). *Legacy: How French-Canadians Shaped North America*. Toronto: Signal.

Putnam, R.D. (2000). *Bowling Alone: The Collapse and Revival of American Community*. New York: Simon & Schuster.

Roberts, C. (2019). Why You Should Ditch New Year's Resolutions for Habit Tracking in 2020. https://www.cnet.com/health/want-to-change-your-life-ditch-new-years-resolutions-for-habit-tracking/

Ross, J.F. (2020). *Two Centuries of French Education in New York: The Role of Schools in Cultural Diplomacy*. New York: TBR.

Ryan, C. (2013). Language Use in the United States: 2011. https://www.census.gov/library/publications/2013/acs/acs-22.html

Saad, L. (2016). France's Favorable Rating in U.S. Zooms to 87%, a New High. https://news.gallup.com/poll/189602/france-favorable-rating-zooms-new-high.aspx

Satell, G., & Popovic, S. (2017). How Protests Become Successful Social Movements. https://hbr.org/2017/01/how-protests-become-successful-social-movements

Schwab, K. (2019). The Global Competitiveness Report 2019. http://www3.weforum.org/docs/WEF_TheGlobalCompetitivenessReport2019.pdf

Sciolino, E. (2020). *The Seine: The River That Made Paris*. New York: W.W. Norton.

Shachtman, T. (2017). *How the French Saved America*. New York: St. Martin's.

Sicot, J., & Brunet, R. (2020). New York, la capitale méconnue de la francophonie. https://lepetitjournal.com/new-york/new-york-la-capitale-meconnue-de-la-francophonie-276512

Solsman, J.E. (2021). Netflix's Lupin Is Its Most Popular Original Show in More Than a Year. https://www.cnet.com/news/netflix-lupin-is-its-most-popular-original-show-in-more-than-a-year-english-french/

Spring, J. (2017). *The Gourmands' Way: Six Americans in Paris and the Birth of a New Gastronomy*. New York: Farrar, Straus, and Giroux.

Statista. (2021). Number of Visitors from France to the United States from 2011 to 2020. https://www.statista.com/statistics/1047826/inbound-travel-from-france-to-the-us/

References

Government of Canada. (2019). Statistics on Official Languages in Canada. (2019). https://www.canada.ca/en/canadian-heritage/services/official-languages-bilingualism/publications/statistics.html

Stearns, P.N. (2008). *Educating Global Citizens in Colleges and Universities: Challenges and Opportunities.* New York: Routledge.

Stein-Smith, K. (2013). *The U.S. Foreign Language Deficit and Our Economic and National Security: A Bibliographic Essay on the U.S. Language Paradox.* Lewiston, NY: Mellen.

The Local. (2016). France Ranked World's Top Cultural Trendsetter. https://www.thelocal.fr/20160120/france-is-worlds-top-trendsetter

The Local. (2018). Macron to Turn Derelict Chateau into Global Beacon for French Language and Culture. https://www.thelocal.fr/20180320/chateau-earmaked-for-global-centre-for-promoting-french-language-and-culture/

The Local. (2019). The Numbers That Tell the Story of the French Language in 2019. https://www.thelocal.fr/20190320/the-numbers-that-tell-the-story-of-the-french-language-in-2019/

Thiery, C. (2020a). A Bridge between Francophone Communities in the Americas. https://france-amerique.com/en/a-bridge-between-francophone-communities-in-the-americas/

Thiery, C. (2018). A French Company in Every State. https://france-amerique.com/en/a-french-company-in-every-u-s-state/

Thiery, C. (2021). Eleven American Dishes with French Origins (Or not...). https://france-amerique.com/en/january-2021/

Thiery, C. (2020b). Ten Legendary French-American Couples. https://france-amerique.com/en/ten-legendary-french-american-couples/

Thuy, N. (2018). Vietnam Holds Huge Business Opportunities for French Companies. http://hanoitimes.vn/vietnam-holds-huge-business-opportunities-for-french-companies-2765.html

Wikipedia. (2021). French Language in the United States. https://en.wikipedia.org/wiki/French_language_in_the_United_States

Wikipedia. (2021). Tony Parker. https://en.wikipedia.org/wiki/Tony_Parker

Tropea, A. (2018). *Adding French to Your English Event.* Toronto, ON. Health Promotion French Language Services Capacity Building Committee. http://en.healthnexus.ca/sites/en.healthnexus.ca/files/resources/hpflscbc_addingfrenchtoy ourevent.pdf

TV5Monde. (2021). Who Are We? http://usa.tv5monde.com/en/about#:~:text=TV5MONDE%20is%20the%20global%20French, reach%201.5%20million%20viewers%20nationwide!

Unger, H.G. (2002). *Lafayette.* New York: Wiley.

U.S. Department of Education. (2021). Teacher Shortage Areas. https://tsa.ed.gov/#/reports

U.S. Department of State. (2021). U.S. Relations with Canada. https://www.state.gov/u-s-relations-with-canada/

U.S. Department of State. (2020). U.S. Relations with France. https://www.state.gov/u-s-relations-with-france/

U.S.News. (2019). The Best Countries: France. https://www.usnews.com/news/best-countries/france

U.S.News. (2021) Louisiana, France Renew Educational, Professional Agreement. https://www.usnews.com/news/best-states/louisiana/articles/2021-02-22/louisiana-france-renew-educational-professional-agreement#:~:text=The%20agreement%20was%20first%20signed,French%20immersion%20programs%20in%20Louisiana.&text=Tens%20of%20thousands%20of%20Louisiana,immersion%20classes%2C%20the%20release%20said

Vermette, D. (2016). Why Are Franco-Americans So Invisible? http://frenchnorthamerica.blogspot.com/2016/03/why-are-franco-americans-so-invisible.html

WGNO Web Desk. (2021). Lt. Gov. Nungesser and CODOFIL re-sign France-Louisiana Accords. (2021). https://wgno.com/news/louisiana/lt-gov-nungesser-and-codofil-re-sign-france-louisiana-accords/

Wikipedia. (2021). French-Americans. https://en.wikipedia.org/wiki/French_Americans#:~:text=Country%2Dwide%2C%20there%20are%20about,the%202011%20American%20Community%20Survey

Wikipedia. (2021). Louisiana Creole. (2021). https://en.wikipedia.org/wiki/Louisiana_Creole

Wikipedia. (2021). Louisiana French. (2021). https://en.wikipedia.org/wiki/Louisiana_French#Preservation_efforts

Willsher. K. (2018). Emmanuel Macron Launches Global Campaign to Promote French Speaking. https://www.theguardian.com/world/2018/mar/20/emmanuel-macron-campaign-french-speaking

Willsher, K. (2021). Ken Follett Gives Book Proceeds to French Cathedral Restoration Fund. https://www.theguardian.com/world/2021/mar/09/ken-follett-gives-book-proceeds-to-french-cathedral-restoration-fund

Wolfestone. (n.d.) Swiss Language Diversity the Key to Success. https://wolfestone.co.uk/insights/blogs/swiss-language-diversity-the-key-to-success

Reuters. (2021). World Bank signs $500 mln Infrastructure Project for Congo's Capital. https://www.reuters.com/world/africa/world-bank-signs-500-mln-infrastructure-project-congos-capital-2021-05-12/

Yechivi, H. (2021). 'The Language Connects Us to Our Identity.' Franco-Americans Strive to Keep the French Language Alive in Maine. https://www.newscentermaine.com/article/news/local/aroostook-county/the-language-connects-us-to-our-identity-franco-americans-strive-to-keep-the-french-alive-in-maine-acadian/97-92df9579-9d8c-452c-8e52-175329e98245

Index

Académie Française 45
Acadians 8, 10, 35, 68
adult learners 71
advocacy 59, 62, 73–74; defined 80; for Francophone culture 82; for French language 77–82; for learning and use of French 103
AEFE *see* Agency for French Education Abroad (AEFE)
Africa 4, 98; aid programs in 44; French language in 45–48; lack of awareness and knowledge of French language and Francophone culture 7–8; trading partner 52
African Union 64
AFSA *see* Association of French Schools in America (AFSA)
Agence de Coopération Culturelle et Technique 40
Agence universitaire de la Francophonie (AUF) 34, 42
Agency for French Education Abroad (AEFE) 42
Alliance Française 4, 11, 22, 29, 31, 41–42, 44, 72, 73, 94
"Ambition Africa" event 52
American Association of Teachers of French (AATF) 70; National French Week 11
American Chamber of Commerce in France (AmCham) 54, 55
American investment, in France 20
American Revolution 3, 13, 15, 16, 21, 23, 27; French ideas in 25

Americans of French ancestry 9, 25, 68, 97
Americans of French heritage 3, 15, 16, 18, 22, 26, 83, 85, 95, 102
Anglophones 58
Araud, Gérard 17–18
Argentina, trading partners 53
Arnault, Bernard 51
Asia 4; French language in 45–48; trading partner 52
Association of French Schools in America (AFSA) 72
attractivité 41, 48, 87, 95

Baker, Josephine 17
Bastille Day celebrations 29
Battle of Québec 34
Beaudry, Prudent 15
Belgium 7, 38, 45, 65, 67
bilingual event, planning 88–89
bilingualism 2, 57, 89; benefits and opportunities of 57; challenges to 60–61; in globalized and interconnected world 58; school-based challenges to 61
Bilingual Revolution 99
Black, Cara 17
Blinken, Antony 17, 19, 23, 75
bootcamp-style immersion programs 71
Boulud, Daniel 17
Brazil, trading partners 53
Brexit 37
Buffett, Warren 15
Business France 52

Index

Call My Agent/Dix pour cent 1, 12, 87
Canada: Francophone businesses 53; Official Languages Act 66; Québec and Francophone Canada 8–9
Carnaval de Québec 8
Cartier, Jacques 15
Cassat, Mary 17
CCI France International 30, 52
Centre de la Francophonie des Amériques (CFA) 11, 34, 40, 47, 82
Chalamet, Timothée 75
Champlain, Samuel de 15
Charter of the French Language (La charte de la langue française) 47
Château de Villers-Cotterêts 39
Child, Julia 17, 31
China 52
"Choose France/*Bienvenue en France*" 52
classroom language learning 63, 93
classroom learners 69
classroom learning 68
CODOFIL *see* Council for the Development of French in Louisiana (CODOFIL)
communication 6, 11, 48, 71; importance of 56; interpersonal 61; in multilingual business environment 50; traditional forms of 22
community-based language learning 94
community building 89, 91–94
competitiveness 50, 51, 58, 65, 67
Cooper, Bradley 17, 75
cosmopolitanism 66
Council for the Development of French in Louisiana (CODOFIL) 10, 29, 41, 54, 64
COVID-19 pandemic 12, 18, 57, 70, 91, 96, 103
creative media 6
creativity 11, 48; language of 39
cultural diversity 42, 59
cultural identity 10, 66, 85; heritage and 75; in North America 2
cultural networks 30–31
Cultural Services of the French Embassy 31
curricular competition 61

Davis, Miles 18
Declaration of Independence 16
Dictionnaire de la langue française 5
Dictionnaire des Francophones 2, 37, 103
digital world 22
Dion, Céline 1, 8
Diouf, Abdou 40
Di Rupo, Elio 46
diversity 59
double majors 62, 77
dual-language immersion programs 18, 26, 27, 38, 48, 71
Duflo, Esther 11

education 31; French as global language of 4, 42–43; issues in 71; traditional forms of 22
ELAN *(École et langues nationales en Afrique)* 42, 63
empowerment 73, 79, 81
English language 58, 59, 61, 75, 76, 80, 86, 98
Enlightenment/*siècle des Lumières* 11
Euronews 39
Europe 4; additional languages 63; French language in 45–48; spoken language in 38
European Day of Languages 65
European exploration 18, 75, 98; of North America 19, 47
European Union (EU) 43–45, 49, 51, 52; multilingualism 65; official language of 37–39

FACC *see* French-American Chamber of Commerce (FACC)
FACE Foundation *see* French-American Cultural Exchange (FACE) Foundation
FACNH *see* Franco-American Centre of New Hampshire (FACNH)
"fashionista" 26, 33
Fisher, MFK 17, 31
Fitzgerald, F. Scott 17
flexibility 94
Florida 10
foreign direct investment (FDI) 45, 50, 56

Index 119

foreign language learning 25, 43, 59; availability of 68; opportunities for 85; shortage of teachers 61
foreign language programs 60, 78; decline in 73
foreign language programs in the elementary schools (FLES) 63, 70
foreign languages: availability of 12; elementary programs in 76; students enrolled in 64
Foster, Jodie 17, 75
Founding Fathers 13, 14, 16, 21, 27, 74
France: economic relations, trade between US and 20; influence and impact on US 21; political relations 19–20; traditional relationship between US and 19; in US 54–55
France 24 39, 43
France Canada Chamber of Commerce 53
France Heritage Foundation of Minnesota 41
France-Louisiana Accords 54, 63–64
France-Vietnam Business Forum 52–53
Franco-American Centre of New Hampshire (FACNH) 11, 41, 82
Franco-Americans 3, 16, 22, 26, 28, 47, 86, 100, 103; authors and artists 11
Franco-Arab Chamber of Commerce 53
francodurabilité 1, 71, 103
Francophiles 3, 12, 41, 43–44, 100, 103
"francophilia" 43
Francophone 3, 25, 41, 100
Francophone Africa 7–8
Francophone businesses 53
Francophone Canada 8–9, 34
Francophone community 26, 35, 90, 95; building of 88–93; development of 3, 91; rebuilding of 93; South Florida 69
Francophone culture 26; advancement of 91; knowledge base on 5, 6; knowledge of 7–8, 12, 76; lack of awareness 7–8; in North America 34–36; resurgence of 74; resurgence of interest in 1; role and importance of 17; role in US cultural identity 17–18; in US 26–28
Francophone organizations, global and regional 40–41
Francophone Radio-Canada 43
Francophones 26, 103
Francophonie 36, 50, 98, 102
francoresponsabilité 1, 71, 103
French *see* French language
French–African partnerships 52
French-American Chamber of Commerce (FACC) 30, 54
French-American Cultural Exchange (FACE) Foundation 31, 71–72
French-American Cultural Foundation 31
French-American relationship: in globalized world 19–24; historical context 13–18
French brands 21–22, 49, 51
French–British conflict 34
French-Canadian businesses 53
French Canadian Legacy Podcast and Blog 11
French Canadians 16, 35
French Chamber of Commerce and Industry 52
French Chamber of Commerce initiatives 71
French Community in Belgium 46
French Creole 8, 10, 28, 36, 44, 68, 86
French Cultural Foundation 23
French dual-language immersion fund 31, 71
French dual-language program 31
French Embassy 29, 72
French Enlightenment/*siècle des Lumières* 13, 15, 16, 21
French fashion 33
"Frenchfluencers" 13, 17, 24, 26
French food/cuisine 14, 31–33
French/Francophone identity 90
French global economic influence 51–54
French heritage language programs 26, 29, 31, 72
French ideas 3, 5, 6, 56; on American culture and on Americans 14; in

Index

American Revolution 25; and creativity 17; and culture 16; of Enlightenment 21; and values 96, 102
French immersion programs 35, 48, 70–71, 96; in Louisiana 66
French investment, in US 20
French Job Fair 53
French language 1; advancement of 91; in Africa, Europe, Asia, and the Americas 45–48; as American language 15–17; and the Americans 28; campaign for 11; and culture in world 41–42; economic impact of 49; famous Americans who speak 29–30; as global and local language 4–10; as global language and competency 43–44; as global language of education 42–43; knowledge of 2, 7–8, 102; lack of awareness 7–8; language for economic trade and cultural exchanges 4; language of education 4; in North America 34–36; resurgence of 74; resurgence of interest in 1; richness and complexity of 3; role and importance of 17; role in US cultural identity 17–18; skills and fluency, role of 93–98; trends and future directions for 83–86; in US 26–28, 54–55; use beyond classroom 81–82; use of 12; in world 38–39; world-wide promotion campaign for 37, 39–40, 98
French language advocacy 77–81; re-inventing 98–101; role of leadership in 92–93; urgency in 80
French language advocates 47, 77, 81; opportunity for 88
French language educators 77, 78
French language initiative 44
French language learning 39, 64, 68, 69, 76, 81, 85, 96, 97; opportunities for 71; re-inventing 98–101; status in US 70–72
French language skills 19, 81; demand for 100; value of 12
French language stakeholder 74, 77, 80, 93–94

French language supporters 47
French lifestyle 22, 50
French reality in America 18
"French Renaissance" 63
French Revolution 16, 21, 36
French "soft power" 1, 19, 21, 37, 39, 40, 48, 51, 96, 102
French start-ups 28
French TV series 1, 14, 87
French wine 32

de Gaulle (President) 35, 47
Germany 49
Global Competitiveness Index 58
global Francophone organizations 40–41
globalization 19, 20, 23, 41, 51, 103
global *lingua franca* 58, 61, 75, 76, 80
de Gramont, Sanche 17
Grand Dérangement 16
de Grasse, François-Joseph (Admiral) 21
Greco, Juliette 18

Haitian community 28, 86
Hemingway, Ernest 17
heritage language community 86
heritage languages 60, 66, 80
heritage learners 60, 69
Hexagone 39
Hollande (President) 23

IFADEM *(L'Initiative francophone pour la formation à distance des maîtres)* 42
immersion programs 6, 63, 64, 68, 71, 76, 77; in public schools 91; shortage of teachers 61
immigrants 36, 69, 95
Institut Français 4, 11, 22, 41, 44, 73
international business 1; language in 38, 39, 49, 51, 56, 96
international influence 21
international media 39
International Olympic Committee 21, 43, 44, 64; official language of 37–39
international trade 49–51
interpersonal communication 61
intrinsic motivation 63

James, Henry 16
Jean, Michaëlle 40
Jefferson, Thomas 31
Johnson, Diane 17
Journée internationale de la Francophonie 10, 39, 40
Juncker, Jean-Claude 45

Kennedy, Jacqueline Bouvier 75
Kerouac, Jack 15, 35, 75
Kerry, John 17, 19, 75
K-12 foreign language learners 77
knowledge: of Francophone culture 12, 76; of French language 2, 102; of heritage languages 66
Kouri-Vini *see* French Creole
K-12 students 61

Lafayette, Marquis de 21, 24
La Francophonie de l'avenir 40
La Loi 101 47
language 31; of culture and diplomacy 3; importance of 56; in international business 38, 39, 49, 51, 56, 96; of international communication 43; role in multilingualism 57; of workplace 55
language advocacy 91
language advocacy activism 92
language education 6, 50, 61, 65, 70
language educators 5, 59, 60, 70, 85, 97
language learners 7, 10, 45, 96
language learning 7, 12, 48, 57, 60, 86, 90, 96; challenges to 60–62, 89; in classroom 93; lack of opportunity for 87–88; outcome 63; predictors of outcome 94; technology in 70; and use of additional languages 66; and use of other languages 58, 62
language policy, development of 62
Languages Act 65
language use 59, 62, 64, 90; challenges to 60–61
Latin America 53
leadership 73–74, 93; role in French language advocacy 92–93; role of Québec 34
Lead with Languages 59

League of Nations 38
Lebovitz, David 17
L'Enfant, Pierre 13, 26, 29
Let's Eat France 31
Le Vent du Nord 11
Lévesque, René 35
Lévy, Bernard-Henri 24
Levy, Marc 17
linguistic diversity 59, 65
Louisiana 9, 10, 15, 21, 35, 63, 72, 75, 86, 99; French immersion programs in 66; *Oui!* Initiative 2, 54, 101
Louis XIV 33
Lupin 1, 6, 12, 24, 74, 83, 87
Luxembourg 7, 38, 45, 65
Lycée Français de New York 72

Macron, Emmanuel 2, 11, 23, 39, 43, 45, 71, 79, 98
Maine 9, 15, 72
Maison Française 29
Many Languages One World Global Youth Forum (MLOW) 64–65
Mastering the Art of French Cooking 31
media 6, 24, 51, 83, 84; creative 6; international 39; online 22, 44, 100; print 44; social 6, 22, 44, 82, 89, 92, 100
Metalious, Grace 15
Middle East 4, 7; aid programs in 44; trading partner 52, 53
MLOW *see* Many Languages One World Global Youth Forum (MLOW)
Mois de la Francophonie 40
Monaco 7, 38, 45, 65
Monroe, Marilyn 18
Montand, Yves 18
mother tongue/fluent speaker 89, 93, 95
motivation 62–63, 79
multilateralism 51
multilingual education programs 63
multilingual environment 37, 79
multilingual immersion programs 48
multilingualism 2, 5–6, 40, 46, 50, 57, 58, 62, 67, 73, 79, 82, 98; development of 62–66
multilingual learning environment 42

multinationals (MNCs) 20
Mushikiwabo, Louise 40

National French Week 70
National Gallery of Art 29
National Language Advocacy
  Day 59
Ndiaye, Sibeth 45
New Hampshire 15
New Hampshire PoutineFest 11
New York City 29, 64
"Night of Ideas/*Nuit des Idées*" 1
No Child Left Behind 61
nongovernmental organizations
  (NGOs) 63
North Africa 7
North America 5; cultural identity
  in 2, 85; European exploration of
  19, 47; French and Francophone
  Culture in 34–36; French colonial
  empire in 16; French language
  supporters and advocates in 47
Nous Foundation 41
la Nouvelle France 14, 16, 27,
  35, 47

Official Languages Act 35,
  47, 66
Olney, Richard 17
online media 22, 44, 100
Ordonnance de Villers-Cotterêts
  (1539) 39, 45
Organisation internationale de la
  Francophonie (OIF) 4, 10, 21, 37,
  38, 40, 43, 44, 53, 54, 64, 72, 75, 82,
  86, 96, 99
Oui! Initiative 2, 54, 101

Paris 6, 11, 13, 14, 17, 20, 21, 32, 33,
  51, 87, 96
Paris Chamber of Commerce 101
Parti Québécois 35
Penney, Louise 8
Pepin, Jacques 17
Perreault, Robert B. 11
Piketty, Thomas 17
plurilingualism 57, 65
preprofessional French language
  skills 71
print media 44
public school immersion programs 94

Québec 40, 47, 53, 55; and
  Francophone Canada 8–9;
  leadership role of 34
Quiet Revolution/*la Révolution*
  tranquille 35, 66

Radio France Internationale (RFI)
  39, 43
regional Francophone organizations
  40–41
Réseau des villes francophones et
  francophiles 40
Revere, Paul 15
revolution bilingue 60
la Révolution bilingue 64
la Révolution tranquille 47
Richard, Zachary 11
de Rochambeau, Jean-Baptiste
  Donatien de Vimeur, comte 21
Romance languages 45, 70
Romney, Mitt 17

Sargent, John Taylor 17
Sarkozy (President) 23
schools: foreign language programs
  in 60; immersion programs in 91;
  languages exist in formal settings
  92; opportunities for French
  education in US 72–73
Sciolino, Elaine 17
self-directed independent learning 89
Senghor, Léopold 40, 45
Servan Schreiber, Jean-Jacques 17
Singapore 58
social media 6, 22, 44, 82, 89, 92, 100
social media influencer (SMI) 92
social movements 73–74, 82, 93–94
social networks 30–31
South Florida, Francophone
  community 69
Stein, Gertrude 17
survivance 1, 35, 103
sustainable French language 77, 78,
  84; development of 91
Sweet Crude 11
Switzerland 7, 38, 45, 46, 58, 65, 67;
  linguistic diversity 65

technology 11, 89, 91; in language
  learning 70
telecommunications 18, 67

terroir 32
Thomas Jefferson Fund 72
Thoreau, Henry David 15
Torres, Jacques 17
traditional foreign language education 6
traditional foreign language programs 62, 68
Tramuta, Lindsey 17
Treaty of Paris (1763) 34, 36
TV5Monde 39, 43, 83

UN Academic Impact 64–65
United Nations 3, 43, 44, 64, 71; official language of 37–39
UN Sustainable Development Goals 67
US: economic relations, trade between France and 20; France and French language in 54–55; French experiences in 29; French language and Francophone culture in 26–28; French language learning status in 70–72; French spoken in 9–10; opportunities for French education in 72–73; political relations 19–20; traditional relationship between France and 19; trends and future directions for the French Language in 83–86
US cultural identity 6; French and Francophone culture role in 17–18
US foreign language deficit 59–62

Vachon, Josée 11
Vermette, David 11
Vermont 15
Verrazzano, Giovanni de 26
Versailles 13, 21, 33

workplace: language of 55; languages exist in formal settings 92; language skills and cultural knowledge 58
World War II 23, 35

For Product Safety Concerns and Information please contact our EU
representative GPSR@taylorandfrancis.com
Taylor & Francis Verlag GmbH, Kaufingerstraße 24, 80331 München, Germany

www.ingramcontent.com/pod-product-compliance
Lightning Source LLC
Chambersburg PA
CBHW051754230426
43670CB00012B/2277